Standards and Procedures for Systems Documentation

Standards and Procedures for Systems Documentation

Andrew W. Poschmann

amacom

American Management Associations

This book is available at a special discount when ordered in bulk quantities. For information, contact Special Sales Department, American Management Associations, Publications Group, 135 West 50th Street, New York, NY 10020.

Library of Congress Cataloging in Publication Data

Poschmann, Andrew W.
Standards and procedures for system documentation.

1. Electronic data processing documentation..
I. Title.
QA76.9.D6P67   1983   001.64'2   83-45207
ISBN 0-8144-7015-7

First Printing

Preface

The purpose of this manual is to provide standards and guidelines for the systematic development, and continued successful operation, of computer-based application systems. In view of the complexities frequently encountered in the data processing function, it is essential to ensure continuity and order in this area of the business, and the book was designed especially with that goal in mind.

The procedures presented here have been developed to satisfy the need for standardized documentation. Such documentation should be prepared as an integral part of system conceptualization, design, and implementation. It will not only ensure the success of the development process but also provide a sound basis for understanding and maintaining the system in the future. This volume includes successfully applied documents that can serve as the standards and procedures manual for the data processing department, with modifications and deletions as deemed appropriate.

The manual also contains a significant section of forms to support day-to-day data processing operations. This area is often neglected, yet it is one of the most vital. The data processing department performs a great number of important transactions for many different business functions. Relying on the memory and availability of a few key operators instead of installing effective standards and procedures places the entire business organization in jeopardy.

Throughout, I have tried to break down complex problems so as to make them understandable, and to provide illustrations demonstrating sound data processing and management practices. I hope that the book will be useful as a working manual, and that it will help improve the data processing function.

Andrew W. Poschmann

About The Author

Andrew W. Poschmann is a systems executive with New York University Medical Center and is a member of the board of advisors of Advanced Management, Inc., a consulting firm based in New York. He has extensive experience in the selection, development, installation, and administration of electronic data processing systems. Mr. Poschmann previously was associated with Ernst & Whinney, Curtiss-Wright Corporation, and A. T. Kearney in consulting and management activities related to information systems.

Mr. Poschmann is a member of the Data Processing Management Association, the Institute of Management Consultants, and the EDP Auditors Foundation. He graduated from the City University of New York and obtained an MBA in finance from Marist College.

Contents

Introduction

This manual is oriented toward all data processing environments: large-scale, mid-size, minis, and micros. Although the complexity of systems and operating environment increases with larger systems, proper documentation of computer applications and procedures is needed regardless of the size and the computer environment.

The advantages of documentation standards are real. Above all, they ensure that people at different levels and departments in the organization will have an accurate and consistent understanding of data processing application systems (payroll, order processing, inventory, and so on). The type and level of detail of documentation vary, of course, for each function. For example, the documentation needs of people concerned with data entry differ from those of people involved in computer program development, which further vary from those of general management--even though all may be involved in the same application system.

The documentation covered here is organized according to the "life cycle" of application systems, illustrated in Table 1:

TABLE 1. THE LIFE CYCLE OF EDP SYSTEMS IMPLEMENTATION AND DOCUMENTATION.

	CONCEPTUAL DESIGN	FUNCTIONAL DESIGN		TECHNICAL DESIGN	OPERATIONAL DOCUMENTATION	PROCEDURAL DOCUMENTATION
	FEASIBILITY	ANALYSIS AND PRELIMINARY DESIGN	SYSTEM DESIGN	PROGRAM AND PROGAM TEST	SYSTEM TRAINING AND TEST	USER ACCEPTANCE
PURPOSE	• Identify Need and Develop an Understanding of the Proposed Project or Support Required	• Identify System Requirements and Prepare a Preliminary System Design	• Refine Preliminary Design Into Final System Design	• Create Detailed Computer Program Specifications, and Create and Test Computer Programs	• Verify that All Programs are Tested as a System that Meets Objectives and Performance Criteria	• Operational Systems in Use
PARTICIPANTS	• Requesting User • Systems Manager or Analyst • Selected User Personnel	• Requesting User • Systems Analyst • Selected User Personnel	• Requesting User • Systems Analyst • Selected User Personnel • Computer Programmer	• Systems Analyst • Computer Programmer	• Systems Analyst • Computer Programmer • Selected User Personnel • EDP Operations Personnel	• Systems Analyst • Selected User Personnel
ACTIVITIES	• Recognize Need • Discuss Situation • Determine Objective and Scope • Quantify Significant Facts • Identify Alternatives • Establish Tentative Priorities • Establish Work Plan (1) • Estimate Time and Costs (1) • Identify Tangible and Intangible Benefits • Prepare Preliminary Implementation Plan	• Gather and Analyze Data • Refine Objectives • Define Performance Criteria • Identify Key Input and Output Documents • Identify System Requirements • Define Features and Capabilities • Evaluate Alternative Designs • Prepare Preliminary System Flowcharts • Identify Subsystems • Identify Interface Points with Other Systems • Identify Hardware, Software, and Communications Requirements • Refine Time and Cost Estimates • Refine Implementation Plan	• Prepare Final Systems Flowchart and Narrative • Determine Required Computer Programs • Draft Forms; CRT and Computer Report Layouts • Identify File Formats and Elements • Identify Editing Criteria • Specify Clerical Support Processes • Specify Data for Conversion • Identify System Test Data • Prepare System Test Plan • Refine Time and Cost Estimates	• Prepare Computer Program Specifications • Complete File Specifications and Design • Create Computer Programs • Create JCL Statements • Develop Program and Job Test Data • Conduct Program Test • Debug Programs • Document Program Tests • Begin EDP Operations Documentation • Update Systems Test Plan	• Complete EDP Operations Documentation • Conduct Systems Test According to Plan • Evaluate System Output • Convert or Create Files • Perform User Training • Prepare Production JCL Statements • Catalog Programs • Begin User Procedural Documentation • Evaluate System and User Readiness • Review Test Results with User • Obtain EDP Operations Group Approval • Obtain User Acceptance of System • Begin User Operation of System	• Complete and Update User Documentation • Identify Areas for Improvement • Provide Additional Training If Needed
DOCUMENTS	• Systems Request • Conceptual Design Proposal • Work Plan • Proposal Cost Estimate Worksheet	• Introduction • System Objective • Scope • Design Concepts • System Flowchart • System Flowchart Narrative • Functional System Flowchart • Functional System Narrative • Operating Environment Impact • Document Analysis Sheet • Glossary of Systems Terms • Progress Report • Report Display Worksheet • Installation Plan • Project Cost Control	• Printer Spacing Chart • CRT Display Formats • File Specification Formats • Data Dictionary • Element Value Tables • Data Control Concepts • Data Security Concepts • Editing Rules • Letter of Intent • List of Required Clerical Desk Instructions • Job Description • System Test Plan • User Training Plan • System Test Data • System Test Results	• System Overview • System Flowchart and Narrative • File Specifications–Contents • File Specifications–Uses • File Specifications–Format • General Description of Programs • Program Function • Program Function Notes • Modification Log • Program Source Listings • Job Control Listings • Information Matrix • Tape and Disk Requirements • Program Test History Record • Program Test Results • Decision Table	• System Overview • System Flowchart and Narrative • Job Instruction Sheet • Job Control Listing • Console Message Listing • Input/Output Schedules • Clerical Desk Instructions • Data Entry Instructions • Remote Terminal Instructions • Remote Job Instructions • Program Release • Request for DP Operations Support • Input/Output Control Procedure • Log of Control Procedures Performed	• Standard Procedure, including: Table of Contents, Subject Index, Procedure, Exhibits • Tape Library File History • Tapes to be Scratched • EDP Operations Schedule • Computer Operations Problem Report • Operations Daily Report
ACTION	• Proceed to Functional Design Upon Approval by Requesting User	• Proceed to System Design Upon Approval by Requesting User	• Design Approved by Systems Manager • Changes in Scope, Time, and Cost Reviewed with Requesting User	• Program Testing Reviewed and Approved by Project Leader and Systems Manager	• Review and Approval by Systems Manager and Requesting User	• Requesting User Review of Performance

(1) *Covers Functional Design phase only on a large project where full effort and costs cannot be determined at this time.*

- o Conceptual design--developing a basic understanding of, and satisfactory approach for, a new system application.
- o Functional design--developing system design specifications.
- o Technical documentation--detail design, program specifications, and testing of new and/or existing systems.
- o Operational documentation--developing operational understanding and instructions.
- o Procedural documentation--developing clerical understanding and instructions.

Proper documentation starts with initial system conceptualization and carries forward through the development cycle. It should not be an after-the-fact, rework, boring endeavor that is inevitably pushed aside or sometimes not done at all.

PURPOSE AND ORGANIZATION OF THE MANUAL

The manual was developed as a working tool. Its purposes are (1) to provide a checklist of activities that must be considered during the development and implementation of systems projects, (2) to describe those activities and identify the sequence in which they should be undertaken, (3) to identify the documentation required during the planning, design, and implementation of systems projects, and (4) to provide detailed instructions for completing each item of required documentation.

For most documents, the following material is included in the book:

1. A blank sample of the document, which may be reproduced for use. The sample appears only when the described document is a preprinted form or report.
2. A blank form keyed, by element, to the instruction sheet.
3. An instruction sheet that identifies and describes each element of the completed document.
4. A completed example of the document. The samples are not to be construed as precise representations of actual case histories. Rather, they are intended to be representative of the type of data that may be furnished.

Within each of the five system-development phases (conceptual design, functional design, technical documentation, operational documentation, and procedural documentation), all the documents prepared during that phase are shown, unless they appear in several phases (in that case they will be referenced, but samples and instructions will appear only for the earliest phase).

A WORD ABOUT MINIS AND MICROS

The distinction between minis and micros is rapidly disappearing. And the distinction between mainframe computers and mini/micros is changing rapidly. With massive growth of small systems, business owners are increasingly expected to handle all phases of data processing themselves, without the aid of computer specialists. The tremendous power of new systems is available at a fraction of the cost that formerly was required for mainframe components.

The availability of packaged software has contributed greatly to the success of the small computer. Little attention is generally paid to the need for operating procedures, controls, scheduling, data, and file content. Just plug it in, load the program and go! However, the concentration of so much information in one place greatly exposes small businesses to loss of control, errors, foul-ups, and misunderstandings. Transfers of cash can get lost, statements may get seasoned with transactions that were never authorized, inventory reporting may not tie in with physical counts. With a few exceptions, every transaction still requires people in the cycle, so potential for human error remains, compounded by the "invisibility" of computer-internal processing. That potential generally expands as personnel changes occur, as they inevitably will in any organization. Just "knowing" what happens, or should happen, is not enough.

Mishaps occur in large established organizations; they are also possible in small firms and can plunge them into confusion. Business journals are replete with tales of large financial institutions and transportation and manufacturing companies that have suffered, sometimes fatally, from computer system failures. It is very difficult to assess an application processing problem quickly when you have no idea where the problem occurs in the system. Auditors traditionally, and rightly so, take a very dim view of nonexistent data processing documentation.

Years ago, when computers were much more expensive, a computer supplier would assign a full-time representative to a purchaser. Today's prices cannot justify such support. Furthermore, many of the software suppliers have neither the resources nor the inclination, nor perhaps even the longevity, to service installed application software. All this emphasizes the need for the user of small computers to have a good knowledge of the software being used. If packaged software is considered, good documentation from the supplier is essential, or else the software is not worth purchasing. Adequate packaged software documentation provides an important base for your own documentation, which will center primarily on clerical and processing procedures.

It should become obvious as you review the standards identified for mini/micro business use that documentation is vital in providing reassurance and stability to the data processing department and its customers.

SOME POINTERS ON DOCUMENTATION

1. Access to system and programming documentation should be controlled. A log of all documents taken out of and returned to the library should be maintained, with a time limit for return.

2. A current version of all documentation should be kept in secure, off-site storage, perhaps in microfiche form, to complement off-site program and data backup.

3. Documentation may take the form of manuals, instruction sheets, or postings on hardware or at a CRT workstation.

4. Documentation can appear on a CRT display to guide an operator through a task.

5. Operator and procedural documentation should tell the user what to do and minimize searching for instructions.

6. Operator and procedural documentation should identify all initial actions and provide clear advice for resolution of problems.

SOME POINTERS ON SYSTEM DEVELOPMENT

1. Large implementation projects should be divided into phases.

2. No phase should exceed six, or at most nine, months.

3. Each phase should be organized into self-contained modules that are guided by the following goals:

    - Rapid attainment of workable results.
    - Identification of useful user enhancements in subsequent phases, based on workable results.
    - User confidence and awareness that progress is occurring.

4. Phases may overlap.

STEPS TOWARD ESTABLISHING A DOCUMENTATION PROGRAM

1. Establish standards enabling uniformity for all development and operation documentation. Standards identify:

   - What documents are necessary
   - Why documents are necessary
   - Who prepares, reviews, and approves the documents
   - How documents are prepared, and what their format and content are
   - When documents are to be prepared

2. Make one person responsible for controlling access to the documentation library (exclusive of active operational and procedural documentation).

3. Ensure adequate space, cabinets, and so on for the library.

4. Inform personnel of new documentation standards and library policies.

5. Consolidate all system documentation into the library.

6. Evaluate existing documentation against a checklist of adopted standards.

7. Select a prototype system to bring documentation up to adopted standards.

8. Establish a plan for correctly documenting existing systems by assigning a percentage of staff time (perhaps 5 percent to 10 percent) to specific systems.

9. Monitor progress against assignments.

10. Monitor use of standards in all new system development projects.

SELECTING THE BEST COMBINATION FOR YOUR PURPOSES

The depth and breadth of data processing systems documentation vary immensely in the real world. Some environments are completely void of any documentation and depend solely upon the individual resources of operational and systems personnel, while other environments produce considerable amounts of documentation--four-inch thick, multiple volumes for conceptual designs alone--that must be maintained by a staff of full-time documentation analysts. There is perhaps a justified need, at times, for both these extremes; however, ordinarily one should strike a balance between disorder and overambitious documentation.

This guide provides simple, proven, straightforward documentation standards that should be extracted and tailored to your individual needs. There is much more here than is expected to be used by any organization. Only those forms that apply specifically to your environment should be considered; different organizations will of course prefer to use different combinations of forms, according to their specific needs. An index of suggested documents for different environments is presented in Table 2.

Table 2. Standards and documents typically used in different environments.

FIGURE NUMBER	DOCUMENT TITLE	MINI/MICRO OWNER USER	MINI/MICRO BUSINESS USE	MAINFRAME "BARE BONES"	MAINFRAME RECOMMENDED	AICPA* RECOMMENDED	OF INTEREST TO MANAGEMENT	MAY BE USEFUL IN MANY SITUATIONS
	CONCEPTUAL DESIGN DOCUMENTATION							
1	Systems Request							•
2	Conceptual Design Proposal				•	•	•	
3	Work Plan				•	•		
4	Proposal Cost Estimate Worksheet				•			
	FUNCTIONAL DESIGN SPECIFICATION							
5	Introduction and System Objectives				•		•	
6	Scope and Design Concepts		•		•	•	•	
7	System Flowchart		•		•	•		
8	System Flowchart Narrative		•		•	•		
9	Functional System Flowchart							•
10	Functional System Flowchart Narrative							•
11	Printer Spacing Chart		•		•	•		
12	CRT Display Format		•		•	•		

*AICPA - American Institute of Certified Public Accountants.

Table 2, *continued*

FIGURE NUMBER	DOCUMENT TITLE	MINI/MICRO OWNER USER	MINI/MICRO BUSINESS USE	MAINFRAME "BARE BONES"	MAINFRAME RECOMMENDED	AICPA* RECOMMENDED	OF INTEREST TO MANAGEMENT	MAY BE USEFUL IN MANY SITUATIONS
	FUNCTIONAL DESIGN SPECIFICATION (continued)							
13	File Specification Record Format, Type 1	•	•	•	•	•		
14	File Specification Record Format, Type 2	•	•	•	•	•		
15	Data Dictionary							•
16	Editing Rules	•	•	•	•	•		
17	Element Value Tables							•
18	Data Control Concepts, Data Security Concepts, and Operating Environment Impact		•	•	•	•	•	
19	Document Analysis Sheet							•
20	Glossary of Systems Terms							•
21	Letter of Intent							•
22	Progress Report							•
23	List of Required Clerical Desk Instructions							•
24	Job Description							•
25	System Test Plan				•			
26	User Training Plan				•			
27	System Test Data				•			
28	System Test Results				•			
29	Installation Plan				•			
30	Report Display Worksheet							•
31	Project Cost Control							•
	TECHNICAL DOCUMENTATION							
32	System Overview				•	•		
33	System Flowchart and Flowchart Narrative			•	•	•		
34	File Specification Contents							•
35	File Specification Usage				•			
36	File Specification Record Format							•
37	General Description of Computer Job/Programs		•		•			
38	Program Function			•	•	•		
39	Program Function Notes			•	•	•		

Table 2, *continued*

FIGURE NUMBER	DOCUMENT TITLE	MINI/MICRO OWNER USER	MINI/MICRO BUSINESS USE	MAINFRAME "BARE BONES"	MAINFRAME RECOMMENDED	AICPA* RECOMMENDED	OF INTEREST TO MANAGEMENT	MAY BE USEFUL IN MANY SITUATIONS
	TECHNICAL DOCUMENTATION (continued)							
40	Modification Log				•	•		
41	Program Source Listing	•	•	•	•	•		
42	Job Control Listing				•			
43	Information Matrix							•
44	Tape and Disk Requirements Sheet							•
45	Program Test History Record							•
46	Program Test Results				•			
47	Decision Table							•
	OPERATIONAL DOCUMENTATION							
48	System Overview, System Flowchart and Flowchart Narrative			•	•	•		
49	Job Instructions, Type 1			•	•	•		
50	Job Instructions, Type 2			•	•	•		
51	Job Control Listing				•	•		
52	Console Message Listing				•	•		
53	Input/Output Schedule				•			
54	Clerical Desk Instructions				•			
55	Data Entry Instructions			•	•			
56	Remote Terminal Instructions		•		•			
57	Remote Job Instructions				•	•		
58	Program Release				•			
59	Request for D.P. Operations Support							•
60	Input/Output Control Procedure				•			
61	Log of Control Procedures Performed		•		•			
62	Tape Library File History							•
63	Tapes To Be Scratched							•
64	EDP Operations Schedule		•		•			
65	Computer Operations Problem Report							•
66	Operations Daily Report				•			

Table 2, *continued*

FIGURE NUMBER	DOCUMENT TITLE	MINI/MICRO OWNER USER	MINI/MICRO BUSINESS USE	MAINFRAME "BARE BONES"	MAINFRAME RECOMMENDED	AICPA* RECOMMENDED	OF INTEREST TO MANAGEMENT	MAY BE USEFUL IN MANY SITUATIONS
	PROCEDURAL DOCUMENTATION							
67	Standard Procedures Manual		•		•	•		
68	Table of Contents		•		•	•		
69	Subject Index		•		•	•		
70	Procedure		•	•	•	•		
71	Exhibits				•	•		

I

CONCEPTUAL DESIGN DOCUMENTATION

Conceptual design documentation is to be used as deemed necessary. Its usefulness depends largely on the size and complexity of the project. Specific components may include:

Systems request (Figure 1)

Conceptual design proposal (Figure 2)

Work plan (Figure 3)

Proposal cost estimate worksheet (Figure 4)

Each of these components is briefly described below. Required forms are illustrated and described in the forms section which follows. The forms section includes a sample of each required form, detailed instructions for preparation, and an example of completed forms. Examples of narrative format are also given.

Systems request. This type of document is generally used in large organizations that require users to specify in writing any requests for new reports, systems, or changes to existing systems.

Conceptual design proposal. As a result of a formal systems request, or oral communication from a user, the data processing department summarizes the background and nature of the request and restates the objectives and scope of the project. The conceptual design proposal is the first level of design in application development. Its purpose is to present an overview of the concepts that a system will use to satisfy its design objectives. The conceptual design proposal is presented in a narrative format using nontechnical language so as to help both user and EDP management to review and approve the proposed systems concepts. The depth of detail may vary; generally, the proposal should convey all details required for the user to understand the work to be performed. Authorization to proceed with development of functional design is based on review and approval of the conceptual design proposal.

Costs, if applicable in a charge-back environment, are also noted. Costs can be for completion of the entire project (if project size allows costing) or for the cost of completion of functional design only. A projected overall anticipated cost is, however, usually desired by prudent management.

It should be noted that a project proposal may consist of a few paragraphs or several hundred pages, depending on scope and magnitude of the project.

Work plan. Presents, in calendar-day sequence, all the tasks required to complete the project and indicates specific individuals responsible for the accomplishment of tasks.

Proposal cost estimate worksheet. Used to develop costs associated with the conceptual design proposal. Presents all the tasks required to complete the project and specific individuals responsible for the accomplishment of tasks. This document is prepared in conjunction with the work plan.

SYSTEMS REQUEST

TO BE COMPLETED BY REQUESTING DEPARTMENT			
TODAY'S DATE	REQUESTED COMPLETION DATE	REQUESTER	DEPARTMENT

REQUEST DESCRIPTION:

INDEX OF ATTACHED DATA	1		4	
	2		5	
	3		6	

OBJECTIVES:

BENEFITS:

TO BE COMPLETED BY SYSTEMS MANAGER			
SYSTEMS RECEIPT ACKNOWLEDGMENT	DATE	SYSTEM AFFECTED	PROJECT NUMBER

TO BE COMPLETED BY SYSTEMS PRIORITY COMMITTEE		
APPROVED BY:	DATE:	PRIORITY DESIGNATION:

TO BE COMPLETED BY COMPUTER SYSTEMS DEPARTMENT			
PROJECT NUMBER	SCHEDULED START DATE	SCHEDULED REVIEW DATE	SCHEDULED COMPLETION DATE

PERSONNEL ASSIGNED

COMMENTS

Figure 1
(Page 2 of 6)

SYSTEMS REQUEST

TO BE COMPLETED BY REQUESTING DEPARTMENT

TODAY'S DATE	REQUESTED COMPLETION DATE	REQUESTER	DEPARTMENT
(1)	(2)	(3)	(4)

REQUEST DESCRIPTION:

(5)

INDEX OF ATTACHED DATA				
	1		4	
	2	(6)	5	
	3		6	

OBJECTIVES:

(7)

BENEFITS:

(8)

TO BE COMPLETED BY SYSTEMS MANAGER

SYSTEMS RECEIPT ACKNOWLEDGMENT	DATE	SYSTEM AFFECTED	REQUEST NUMBER
(9)	(10)	(11)	(12)

TO BE COMPLETED BY SYSTEMS PRIORITY COMMITTEE

APPROVED BY:	DATE:	PRIORITY DESIGNATION:
(13)	(14)	(15)

TO BE COMPLETED BY COMPUTER SYSTEMS DEPARTMENT

PROJECT NUMBER	SCHEDULED START DATE	SCHEDULED REVIEW DATE	SCHEDULED COMPLETION DATE
(16)	(17)	(18)	(19)

PERSONNEL ASSIGNED

(20)

COMMENTS

(21)

INSTRUCTIONS FOR FORM: SYSTEMS REQUEST

DEFINITION OF EACH ELEMENT:

KEY	ELEMENT/CONTENT
1.	Today's Date Date this request is initiated.
2.	Requested Completion Date Date requester desires work completed.
3.	Requester Name of requester.
4.	Department Requester's department.
5.	Request Description Specific, concise description of request.
6.	Index of Attached Data Listing of documents supporting or clarifying the request.
7.	Objectives The anticipated results or goals that would be achieved through the accomplishment of the request.
8.	Benefits The benefits that would accrue to the organization as a result of implementing the request.
9.	Systems Receipt Acknowledgment Signature of receiver.
10.	Date Date of receipt.

INSTRUCTIONS FOR FORM: SYSTEMS REQUEST--Continued

DEFINITION OF EACH ELEMENT:

KEY **ELEMENT/CONTENT**

11. System Affected

Relates the system affected, i.e., payroll, accounts payable, etc. If a new system is required, it would be so noted.

12. Request Number

Number assigned for control purposes.

13. Approved By

Signature of Systems Priority Committee representative indicating committee approval.

14. Date

Date request approved by the Committee.

15. Priority Designation

The priority assigned to the request by the Systems Priority Committee.

16. Project Number

Project number assigned to approved request.

17. Scheduled Start Date

Date work is scheduled to start on request.

18. Scheduled Review Date

Date for scheduled project review.

19. Scheduled Completion Date

Date scheduled to be completed.

INSTRUCTIONS FOR FORM: SYSTEMS REQUEST--Continued

DEFINITION OF EACH ELEMENT:

KEY	ELEMENT/CONTENT
20.	Personnel Assigned Computer systems department personnel assigned to the project.
21.	Comments Miscellaneous comments. May include disposition of project.

Figure 1

SYSTEMS REQUEST **EXAMPLE** (Page 6 of 6)

TO BE COMPLETED BY REQUESTING DEPARTMENT

TODAY'S DATE	REQUESTED COMPLETION DATE	REQUESTER	DEPARTMENT
Sept. 15, 19XX	Mid-year 19XX	S. Astrol	Plant Maintenance

REQUEST DESCRIPTION:

Provide information on equipment component life history

INDEX OF ATTACHED DATA				
	1	Report on equipment breakdowns	4	
	2	Report on comparative manpower requirements	5	
	3	Summary of equipment availability	6	

OBJECTIVES:

To schedule equipment maintenance based on component life rather than at breakdown.

BENEFITS:

Increase the availability and utilization of equipment.
Level maintenance manpower requirements.

TO BE COMPLETED BY SYSTEMS MANAGER

SYSTEMS RECEIPT ACKNOWLEDGMENT	DATE	SYSTEM AFFECTED	PROJECT NUMBER
B. Williams	9/18/XX	Equipment component	145

TO BE COMPLETED BY SYSTEMS PRIORITY COMMITTEE

APPROVED BY:	DATE:	PRIORITY DESIGNATION:
A. Donnate	9/29/XX	#4

TO BE COMPLETED BY COMPUTER SYSTEMS DEPARTMENT

PROJECT NUMBER	SCHEDULED START DATE	SCHEDULED REVIEW DATE	SCHEDULED COMPLETION DATE
2004	10/12/XX	10/14/XX	10/16/XX

PERSONNEL ASSIGNED

G. Kyle

COMMENTS

INSTRUCTIONS FOR FORM: CONCEPTUAL DESIGN PROPOSAL

DEFINITION OF EACH ELEMENT:

KEY **ELEMENT/CONTENT**

1. Cover Letter (Optional)

   To be used when proposal is lengthy or detailed.

2. Background

   The nature of the assistance requested is described, including general background information on the situation which led to the request. Restates the symptoms, problems, and cause that were presented in preliminary meetings and discussions with the user.

3. Synopsis (Optional)

   Summarizes the key points identified during data gathering. The following subtopics may be included:

   a. Present operation of system.

   b. Organizational attitude toward present system.

   c. Evaluation of probable management involvement.

4. Objective

   States the objective to be achieved at this time.

5. Method of Approach

   Summarizes the method, or methods, of approach that may be used. Sufficient detail of various alternatives is presented to relate the benefits of each to the cost.

6. Economic Evaluation (Optional)

   Potential benefits are quantified and presented. Indicate cost of systems, programming, and computer test time where applicable (usually charge-back installations). Anticipated elapsed time required must also be shown.

Note: The document is free-form.

EXAMPLE

To:	Mr. J. Scolozi	Date:	April 16, 19XX
Subject:	Supplies Inventory System	Place:	Computer Systems Department
	(1)	cc:	Mr. J. A. Barr

Attached is detailed information regarding the Supplies Inventory System which we discussed last week.

In brief, development will cost $20,000 with an additional $5,000 for computer test time.

If you have any questions regarding the project, or if we have not clarified any points to your satisfaction, please contact me or D. Strom at your convenience.

As soon as we have approval, we will commence analysis.

J. Able

Att.

Note: This example includes a cover letter, which should be used when proposal is lengthy or detailed.

EXAMPLE

Figure 2
(Page 3 of 5)

CONCEPTUAL DESIGN PROPOSAL
FOR A
SUPPLIES INVENTORY SYSTEM

BACKGROUND (2)

This conceptual design specification describes the proposed Supplies Inventory Control System. The request for this analysis was initiated by the Manager, Office Services, and approved by the EDP Steering Committee on July 16, 19XX. The study was based on the need to provide better service to all areas of the company while at the same time controlling increasing office-supplies expenses.

The design specification includes the objectives, scope, technical considerations, and cost/benefit analysis for this application.

Costs of consumable office supplies have been increasing at a rate of nearly 100 percent each year for the past three years. It has been determined that a significant part of this expense has been incurred as various departments have assimilated their own supplies inventory. In order to control these expenses, a central office supplies inventory has been established within the Office Services Department.

SYNOPSIS (3)

The Supplies Inventory System is being developed to support the activities of the office supplies inventory function. This system will provide management with inventory stock-on-hand and reorder levels that will interface directly with the Inter-Department Billing System so that user departments will be charged directly for supplies drawn.

OBJECTIVE (4)

This system is being developed to process data on consumable office supplies inventory and consumption. Inventories of capitalized items such as typewriters and office furniture will be excluded from this system. Special forms, stationery, or other supplies unique to a department or function may be inventoried and controlled under this system at the discretion of user departments, pending the development of a Centralized Supplies Purchasing System. Once the latter system is implemented, all consumable office supplies will be inventoried and disbursed through the central storeroom.

This system is based on three information sources:

1. Purchase order placed with vendor.
2. Receiving document for incoming supplies.
3. Supply requisition for which material is issued.

A computer record will be established for each of the items identified as a common supply item. As each of these three documents is processed through the system, the record for each item will be updated via a CRT terminal located in the supply room. Reports on inventory levels and reorder positions will be published weekly in a batch processing cycle. Input to the Inter-Department Billing System will be generated automatically at the month-end cutoff.

METHOD OF APPROACH (5)

All supplies will be disbursed through the central supplies storeroom, and transactions will be recorded through the central supplies data input and display terminal.

Approximately 20 purchases, 20 receipts, and 150 supplies requisition transactions will be entered daily. No measurable adverse impact on the on-line processing network is anticipated.

The supplies inventory data base will contain a master record for each of an estimated 250 supply items.

Hardware requirements for this Supplies Inventory System are minimal. The data base requires an estimated 40,000 bytes of on-line disk storage. The transaction file requires 10,000 bytes of on-line disk storage for a day's activity and tape file capacity for a month's activity. One CRT terminal will provide adequate transaction processing capability in the supplies storeroom. Direct access to the data base is required during the central storeroom operating hours, 8:30 a.m. to 4:30 p.m., Monday through Friday.

The data base required for this Supplies Inventory System is to be developed from available records at the scheduled year-end physical inventory. These records will be keypunched and an initial file created. Each record will include the description of the item, unit of purchase and issue, price, and quantity. The Manager, Office Services, will be responsible for the quality of the initial data conversion.

ECONOMIC EVALUATION (6)

It is expected that implementation of this system will curtail the growth of the "unofficial" office supply inventories being maintained throughout the company, and provide more accurate records of supplies inventory level and consumption, in addition to controlling costs of supplies through direct billing. You have estimated cost savings of $6,000, or 15 percent of current expenses, in the first year, with an increase to $8,000 in subsequent years.

Preliminary development efforts are estimated at $25,000, of which $20,000 will be incurred for systems and programming, with the balance for computer test time. Operating costs at current computer center rates are projected to be $400 per month. We anticipate an elapsed time for implementation of about four months.

R. Jones
Systems Analyst

J. Able
Manager of Systems

Figure 3
(Page 1 of 5)

WORK PLAN

DATE PREPARED: ____________

PREPARED BY: ____________

PROJECT NAME: ____________ PROJECT NO.: ____________

NO.	TASK	PRIME RESPONSIBILITY	ASSIGNED TO	START DATE		STOP DATE		ELAPSED TIME		MAN-DAYS	
				SCH	ACT	SCH	ACT	SCH	ACT	SCH	ACT

Figure 3
(Page 2 of 5)

WORK PLAN

(1) DATE PREPARED: ____________

(2) PREPARED BY: ____________

(3) PROJECT NAME: ____________

(4) PROJECT NO.: ____________

NO.	TASK	PRIME RESPONSIBILITY	ASSIGNED TO	START DATE		STOP DATE		ELAPSED TIME		MAN-DAYS	
				SCH	ACT	SCH	ACT	SCH	ACT	SCH	ACT
(5)	(6)	(7)	(8)	(9)	(10)	(11)	(12)	(13)	(14)	(15)	(16)

INSTRUCTIONS FOR FORM: WORK PLAN

DEFINITION OF EACH ELEMENT:

KEY	ELEMENT/CONTENT
1.	Date Prepared The date that the work plan was prepared.
2.	Prepared By Person who prepared the work plan.
3.	Project Name Name assigned to project.
4.	Project Number Number assigned to project.
5.	Number The number assigned to a project task.
6.	Task Description of task.
7.	Prime Responsibility The individual assigned responsibility for successful completion of the task.
8.	Assigned to The individuals assigned to complete the task.
9.	Start Date--Scheduled The date the task is scheduled to be started.
10.	Start Date--Actual The date the task was actually started.

INSTRUCTIONS FOR FORM: WORK PLAN--Continued

DEFINITION OF EACH ELEMENT:

KEY	ELEMENT/CONTENT
11.	Stop Date--Scheduled The date the task is scheduled to be completed.
12.	Stop Date--Actual The date the task was actually completed.
13.	Elapsed Time--Scheduled The number of calendar days scheduled for completion of the task.
14.	Elapsed Time--Actual The actual number of calendar days required to complete the task.
15.	Man-Days--Scheduled The number of people-days scheduled for completing the task.
16.	Man-Days--Actual The actual number of people-days required to complete the task.

Figure 3
(Page 5 of 5)

EXAMPLE

WORK PLAN

DATE PREPARED: 11/17/XX

PREPARED BY: E. Nixdorf

PROJECT NAME: Supplies Inventory System

PROJECT NO.: 7069

NO.	TASK	PRIME RESPONSIBILITY	ASSIGNED TO	START DATE		STOP DATE		ELAPSED TIME		MAN-DAYS	
				SCH	ACT	SCH	ACT	SCH	ACT	SCH	ACT
1.	Orientation	J. Able	R. Jones	2/1		2/1		1		2	
2.	Survey Current Operation; Gather Forms, Documents	R. Jones	-	2/5		3/5		30		8	
3.	Systems Design	R. Jones	N. Green	2/20		3/20		30		15	
4.	User Review	R. Jones	-	3/20						1	
5.	Program Design, Development	R. Jones	N. Green	3/15		4/15		30		20	
6.	Program Testing	N. Green	-	4/15		5/10		25		10	
7.	Data Conversion, System Testing	R. Jones	N. Green	5/10		5/30		20		6	
8.	Training	R. Jones	-	5/20		5/30		10		5	
9.	Parallel Operation	R. Jones	-	5/30		6/30		30		4	
10.	Complete Documentation	R. Jones	N. Green	6/15		7/15		30		15	

Figure 4
(Page 1 of 5)

PROPOSAL COST ESTIMATE WORKSHEET

DEPARTMENT	PROJECT TITLE	REVISION	PAGE OF

PREPARED BY	DATE	APPROVED BY	DATE	PROJECT NUMBER & SUFFIX

TASK NO.	TASK DESCRIPTION	PERSONNEL DAYS								TOTALS
	TOTAL DAYS									
	STD. RATES									
	TOTAL STD. COST									

SUMMARY

TOTAL STD. COST FEES	
ALLOWANCE	
PROPOSED COST	
EXPENSES	

ALLOWANCE EXPLANATION & COMMENTS

Figure 4
(Page 2 of 5)

PROPOSAL COST ESTIMATE WORKSHEET

DEPARTMENT (1)	PROJECT TITLE (2)	REVISION (3)	PAGE OF (4)
PREPARED BY (5) DATE (6)	APPROVED BY (7) DATE (8)	PROJECT NUMBER & SUFFIX (9)	

TASK NO.	TASK DESCRIPTION	PERSONNEL DAYS								TOTALS
(10)	(11)	(12)								(13)
	(14) TOTAL DAYS									
	(15) STD. RATES									
	TOTAL STD. COST (16)									

SUMMARY (17)

TOTAL STD. COST FEES	
ALLOWANCE	
PROPOSED COST	
EXPENSES	

ALLOWANCE EXPLANATION & COMMENTS

(18)

INSTRUCTIONS FOR FORM: PROPOSAL COST ESTIMATE WORKSHEET

DEFINITION OF EACH ELEMENT:

KEY	ELEMENT/CONTENT
1.	Department Name of the department to be served.
2.	Project Title Name associated with the proposal.
3.	Revision Revision number if applicable.
4.	Page Page number, i.e., 1 of 3.
5.	Prepared By Name of preparer.
6.	Date Date of preparation.
7.	Approved By Name of person who approved the estimate.
8.	Date Date of approval.
9.	Project Number Number assigned to the project.
10.	Task Number Number assigned to each task.
11.	Task Description Description of task to be performed.

INSTRUCTIONS FOR FORM: PROPOSAL COST ESTIMATE WORKSHEET--Continued

DEFINITION OF EACH ELEMENT:

KEY	ELEMENT/CONTENT
12.	Personnel Days Identification of personnel who may be assigned plus estimate of number of days that may be required for each person, by task.
13.	Totals Extension of the number of days anticipated for each task.
14.	Total Days Sum of days for each person.
15.	Standard Rates Daily rate applied to each person.
16.	Total Standard Cost Product of standard rate by number of days per person.
17.	Summary Recap of total standard costs plus any allowances applied for increasing or decreasing proposed cost. Proposed cost is noted, plus any outside expenses which are anticipated.
18.	Allowance Explanation and Comments Any comments pertinent to proposal cost estimating.

Figure 4
(Page 5 of 5)

EXAMPLE

PROPOSAL COST ESTIMATE WORKSHEET

DEPARTMENT	PROJECT TITLE	REVISION	PAGE
Office Services	Supplies Inventory	-	1 OF 1

PREPARED BY	DATE	APPROVED BY	DATE	PROJECT NUMBER & SUFFIX
E. Nixdorf	11/23/XX	R. Barrett	11/26/XX	7069

TASK NO.	TASK DESCRIPTION	PERSONNEL DAYS								TOTALS
		E.N.	R.J.	N.G.	Eqpt. Time					
1.	Orientation	1	1							2
2.	Survey Current Operation		8							8
3.	System Design		8	7						15
4.	User Review		1							1
5.	Program Design, Development		3	17						20
6.	Program Testing			10						10
7.	Data Conversion, System Testing		2	4						6
8.	Training		5							5
9.	Parallel Operation		2	2						4
10.	Complete Documentation		10	5						15
11.	Program Test, Conversion Machine Time at									
	96 hours ÷ 8 = 12 days				12					12
	TOTAL DAYS	1	40	45	12					98
	STD. RATES	275	250	200	400					
	TOTAL STD. COST	275	10,000	9,000	4,800					24,075

SUMMARY

TOTAL STD. COST FEES	24,075
ALLOWANCE	925
PROPOSED COST	25,000
EXPENSES	None

ALLOWANCE EXPLANATION & COMMENTS

Allowance for overrun

II

FUNCTIONAL DESIGN SPECIFICATION

The functional design specification is the second level of design (following the conceptual design specification) in application development. It is a comprehensive application description written from the user's point of view in nontechnical terms. It includes descriptions of all source data, processing, and system output. After approval by the intended users of the system output, the documentation is used by the technical staff for implementation.

Following are the required elements in a functional design specification for a new application's development. Although not every component may apply to every project, all those which are relevant must be included.

Introduction (Figure 5)

System objectives (Figure 5)

Scope (Figure 6)

Design concepts (Figure 6)

System flowchart (Figure 7)

System flowchart narrative (Figure 8)

Functional system flowchart (Figure 9)

Functional system flowchart narrative (Figure 10)

Printer spacing chart (Figure 11)

CRT display format (Figure 12)

File specifications--record format, Type 1 (Figure 13)

File specifications--record format, Type 2 (Figure 14)

Data dictionary (Figure 15)

Editing rules (Figure 16)

Element value tables (Figure 17)

Data control concepts (Figure 18)

Data security concepts (Figure 18)

Operating environment impact (Figure 18)

Document analysis sheet (Figure 19)

Glossary of systems terms (Figure 20)

Letter of intent (Figure 21)

Progress report (Figure 22)

List of required clerical desk instructions (Figure 23)

Job description (Figure 24)

System test plan (Figure 25)

User training plan (Figure 26)

System test data (Figure 27)

System test results (Figure 28)

Installation plan (Figure 29)

Report display worksheet (Figure 30)

Project cost control (Figure 31)

The following sections briefly describe each of the components which may be included in the functional design specification. The forms section includes an example of each of these components. Where appropriate, samples of required and detailed instructions for their preparation are also included.

Introduction. The introduction is a brief narrative providing an overview of the application. It also outlines the contents of the functional design specification. Any significant differences between the conceptual design and the functional-design concepts, system objectives, or scope which may arise from the more detailed analysis performed at this level must be noted in this section.

System objectives. This is a statement of the intended goals of the system. A brief background statement may be included, if appropriate.

Scope. The limits of the application are stated in this section. Identification of subjects related to the application but excluded from this design is an important part of the definition of project scope.

Design concepts. The statement of design concepts is a summary of the system functions from the user's point of view. It describes, briefly, data sources, on-line and batch processing concepts, data base files supported, and types of system output.

System flowchart. The system flowchart is a graphic representation of a system's processing steps. The system flow begins with relevant source documents and data-entry steps. Each processing, data sequencing, and data base backup program is then represented, illustrating all files, reports, and on-line displays, as appropriate.

The charts are intended to present the logical flow of program steps within the system. Each subsystem of related programs should be presented on a separate flowchart. Independent, stand-alone programs should be shown as such.

System flowchart narrative. A function description is required for each of the program processing steps in the system flowcharts. Each description includes:

Input--a list of input data files.

Processing--a description of principal processing actions performed in this step. Detailed program logic specifications are not required at this level. However, unique calculations or unusual processing routines must be clearly documented in narrative or other format, as appropriate.

Output--a list of program output, including (1) data files, (2) updated data base files, and (3) reports.

Functional system flowchart. The functional system flowchart is useful to graphically present the flow and concept of processing for the proposed system. The format used may vary depending on the nature of the system. However, there are some standard techniques which should be followed:

- The flowchart may be drawn at different levels of detail. The level of detail should be more precise in those areas which are essential to the operation of the system.

- Key reports, input documents, and organization units should be identified.

- Processes, not programs or clerical desk instructions, should be identified.

Functional system flowchart narrative. This is used to describe the events and processes that are graphically presented on the functional system flowchart. The narrative must be cross-referenced to the flowchart.

Printer spacing chart. All printed reports must be documented on report layout forms. Descriptions of data elements which are the result of calculations or which are otherwise not self-explanatory must be included in the program description associated with the report.

Report layouts must indicate report heading, including title, and program ID; date the report is printed with "As of" date, page number, and period included, if applicable; column headings; line skipping requirements; total levels; and all line formats, including detail data lines, total lines, and control total lines.

CRT display formats. All operator-guidance, file-inquiry, and data-entry displays must be documented on screen layout forms. Descriptions of data elements which are the result of calculations or are otherwise not self-explanatory must be included in the program function associated with the display.

File specifications--record format, Types 1 and 2. Permanent and transient file layouts must be documented on standard file specification forms. Each file specification includes every data element, by record type, in the file, and includes the name of each element, its size, its position in the record, its type, and, if required for clarification, descriptive comments. Files will be documented in this fashion only when they are first created. Subsequent use of the same file in other systems does not necessitate redoing this form. New-project documentation should merely refer to the existing system.

Data dictionary. The data dictionary is an alphabetical listing of the data elements used in the system. It includes, for each entry, the standard name or "label" assigned by the program designer (and used in all program references to this element) and the size and character (picture) of the element.

Editing rules. This document describes the edit criteria applied to all data elements, whether on-line or batch. The elements and corresponding edit rules are recorded on the form.

Element value tables. The valid values for coded data elements are recorded on element value table worksheets. A separate page is used for each element.

Data control concepts. Provision must be made at this level of design for data control points and audit trails. This includes planning of interfaces with external controls and balances. The data control method is summarized in narrative form.

Data security concepts. Consideration must be given at this level of design to identifying authorized data sources, terminals, and data recipients in on-line environments. Authorized users must be documented in keeping with the overall data processing network security system. Any unusual operations required as a result of data security provisions must be documented in narrative form.

Operating environment impact. Every application is developed and executed in conjunction with other production applications. Consideration must be given to the impact of new applications on the existing operating environment. The impact of any proposed on-line applications on the response time of existing systems should be estimated and included.

Document analysis sheet. This document is used to describe the purposes, the various uses, the method of preparation, and the distribution for a form or report. This sheet may be used for both existing and proposed systems.

Glossary of systems terms. This document is used to document key words, terms, and phrases associated with a system.

Letter of intent. Used to advise computer and communications vendors of the intent to purchase equipment under specified conditions. This letter places the user in the manufacturer's backlog queue. Company letterhead is used.

Progress report. Provides a means for reporting the status, progress, and problems of large-scale system projects.

List of required clerical desk instructions. A list of all clerical desk instructions that will have to be prepared.

Job description. Presents the purpose, organizational relationship, and specific major duties of each position.

System test plan. Records all the planned activities and events that must take place during the systems test phase.

User training plan. Presents a detailed plan covering the who, what, when, and where of user training for a new system.

System test data. Identifies the various source documents and other inputs to the system being tested and describes the output of a successful test.

System test results. Provides samples of actual output of the systems test.

Installation plan. Presents the steps required to install the system and identifies the personnel responsible for these steps.

Report display worksheet. Useful to identify report format, use, controls, and authorization.

Project cost control. Enables week-to-week tracking of hours spent and dollars incurred by each member of a project team. Also provides a cumulative recap for each period to relate current expenditures against a predefined budget.

EXAMPLE Figure 5

FUNCTIONAL DESIGN SPECIFICATION

SUPPLIES INVENTORY SYSTEM

INTRODUCTION

This functional design specification describes the Supplies Inventory System. The development of this design level was approved by the Manager, Office Services, and the EDP Steering Committee on August 27, 19XX, based on the conceptual design specification of August 18, 19XX. This document is a comprehensive description of the system to be developed.

SYSTEM OBJECTIVES

Costs of consumable office supplies have been increasing at a rate of nearly 100% each year for the past three years. It has been determined that a significant part of this expense has been incurred as various departments have assimilated their own supplies inventory. In order to control these expenses, a central office supplies inventory has been established within the Office Services Department.

The Supplies Inventory System is being developed to support the activities of the office supplies inventory function. This system will provide management with inventory stock-on-hand and reorder levels that will interface directly with the Inter-Department Billing System so that user departments will be charged directly for supplies drawn.

EXAMPLE

Figure 6

SCOPE

This system is being developed to process data on consumable office supplies inventory and consumption. Inventories of capitalized items such as typewriters and office furniture will be excluded from this system. Special forms, stationery, or other supplies unique to a department or function may be inventoried and controlled under this system at the discretion of user departments, pending the development of a Centralized Supplies Purchasing System. Once the latter system is implemented, all consumable office supplies will be inventoried and disbursed through the central storeroom.

DESIGN CONCEPTS

This system is based on three information sources:

1. Purchase order placed with vendor.
2. Receiving document for incoming supplies.
3. Supply requisition for which material is issued.

A computer record will be established for each of the items identified as a common supply item. As each of these three documents is processed through the system, the record for each item will be updated via a CRT terminal located in the supply room. Reports on inventory levels and reorder positions will be published weekly in a batch processing cycle. Input to the Inter-Department Billing System will be generated automatically at the month-end cutoff.

Figure 7
(Page 1 of 4)

SYSTEM FLOWCHART

SYSTEM		DATE
PROCEDURE	PREPARED BY	PAGE OF

Figure 7
(Page 2 of 4)

SYSTEM FLOWCHART

SYSTEM (1)		DATE (4)
PROCEDURE (2)	PREPARED BY (3)	PAGE (5) OF

(6)

INSTRUCTIONS FOR FORM: SYSTEM FLOWCHART

DEFINITION OF EACH ELEMENT:

KEY	ELEMENT/CONTENT
1.	System Name of the major system being charted.
2.	Procedure Name of the subsystem being charted.
3.	Prepared By Name of person preparing the document.
4.	Date Date that this chart was prepared.
5.	Page Indicate the page sequence and total number.
6.	Flowchart Detail Using symbols, presents, a graphic representation of the system's processing steps.

Figure 7
(Page 4 of 4)

EXAMPLE

SYSTEM FLOWCHART

SYSTEM		DATE
OFFICE SERVICES		8/20/XX
PROCEDURE: SUPPLIES INVENTORY SYSTEM	PREPARED BY: G. Jones	PAGE: 1 OF 1

DAILY PROCESSING--ON LINE

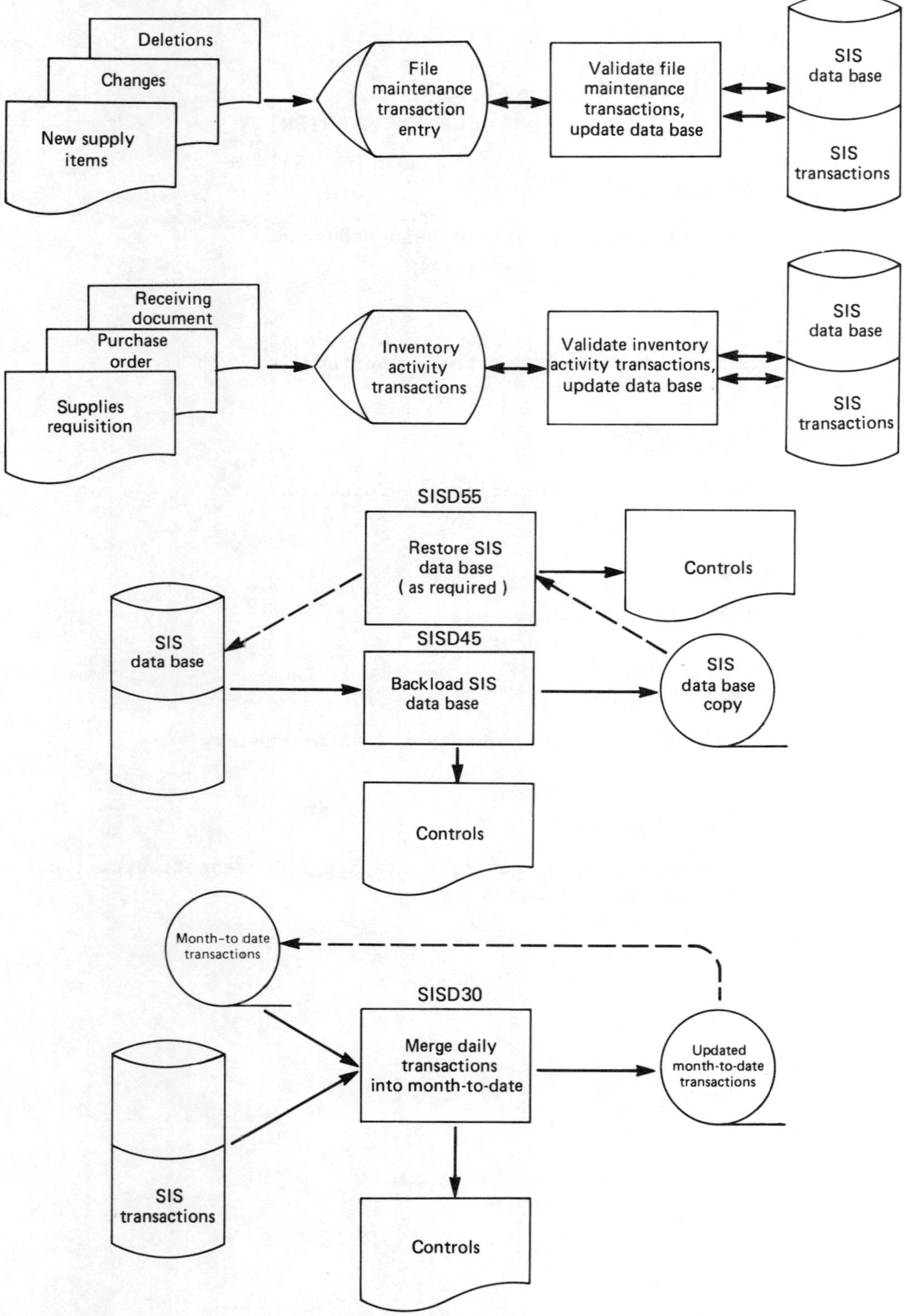

INSTRUCTIONS FOR FORM: SYSTEM FLOWCHART NARRATIVE

DEFINITION OF EACH ELEMENT:

KEY	ELEMENT/CONTENT
1.	Date Prepared The date the narrative was prepared.
2.	System Name assigned to the system.
3.	Procedure Name assigned to the procedure.
4.	Prepared By Name of preparer.
5.	Input Files used in the procedure.
6.	Processing Narrative of processes to occur. Should be logically separated by specific functions.
7.	Output Reports or output generated by the process.

EXAMPLE

Figure 8
(Page 2 of 3)

SYSTEM FLOWCHART NARRATIVE

(1.)	DATE:	August 20, 19XX
(2.)	SYSTEM:	Supplies Inventory System
(3.)	PROCEDURE:	Validate and update Supplies Issue and Receipt Transactions
(4.)	PREPARED BY:	G. Jones
(5.)	INPUT:	Current SIS Data Base
		Current SIS Transaction File
		Purchase Order, Receipt, and Store Requisition Transactions
(6.)	PROCESSING:	PURCHASE-ORDER TRANSACTION

Match supply item ID number to SIS Master Record.

If record is on file and is Active:

- o Validate transaction according to edit rules.
- o Validate control total.
- o Add open-order amount to "Quantity on Order" data element in master record.
- o Add open-order amount to "Ordered to Date" data element in master record.
- o Record transaction on Transaction File.

If record is not on file or is not Active:

- o Display "Not on File--Reject" message.

RECEIPT-OF-SUPPLY-ITEM TRANSACTION

Match supply item ID number to SIS Master Record.

If record is on file and is Active:

- o Validate transaction according to edit rules.
- o Validate control total.
- o Subtract quantity received from "Quantity on Order" data element in master record.

EXAMPLE

- o Add quantity received to "Quantity on Hand" data element in master record.
- o Record transaction on Transaction File.

If record is not on file or is not Active:

- o Display "Not on File--Reject" message.

STORES-REQUISITION TRANSACTION

Match supply item ID number to SIS Master Record

If record is on file and is Active:

- o Validate transaction according to edit rules
- o Validate control total.
- o Subtract quantity issued from "Quantity On Hand" data element in master record.
- o Record transaction on Transaction File.

If record is not on file or is not Active:

- o Display "Not on File-Reject" message.

(7.) OUTPUT: Control Reports

Exceptions

Inter-Department Billing Support Records

Figure 9
(Page 1 of 4)

FUNCTIONAL
SYSTEM FLOWCHART

SYSTEM NAME: ____________________ DATE: ____________________

PROJECT NUMBER: ____________________ PREPARED BY: ____________________

**FUNCTIONAL
SYSTEM FLOWCHART**

(1)

(2)
SYSTEM NAME: ____________________

(3)
PROJECT NUMBER: ____________________

DATE: ____________________

(4)
PREPARED BY: ____________________

(5)

INSTRUCTIONS FOR FORM: FUNCTIONAL SYSTEM FLOWCHART

DEFINITION OF EACH ELEMENT:

KEY	ELEMENT/CONTENT
1.	Date The date the flowchart was prepared.
2.	System Name Name assigned to the system.
3.	Project Number Number assigned to the project.
4.	Prepared By Person who prepared the flowchart.
5.	Flowchart Detail Using symbols, presents, the operational flow of information through the system.

Figure 9
(Page 4 of 4)

EXAMPLE

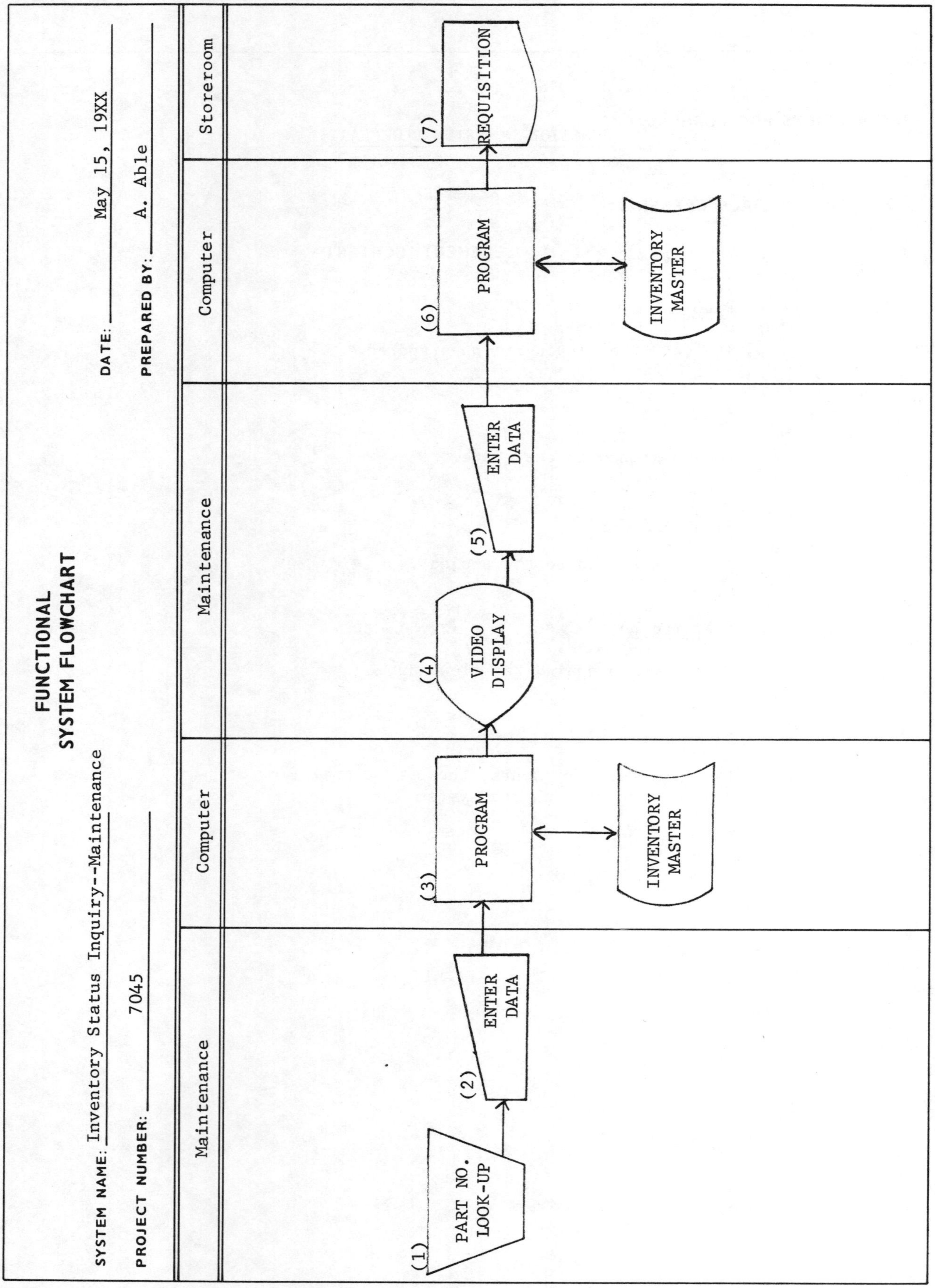

INSTRUCTIONS FOR FORM: FUNCTIONAL SYSTEM FLOWCHART NARRATIVE

DEFINITION OF EACH ELEMENT:

KEY	ELEMENT/CONTENT
1.	Date Prepared The date the narrative was prepared.
2.	System Name Name assigned to the system.
3.	Project Number Number assigned to the project.
4.	Prepared By Person who prepared the flowchart.
5.	Narrative Detail Identifies: a. Organizational placement of responsibilities. b. Key input documents, output reports, and files by name. c. All other documents and reports in general terms. d. Decision logic and significant data processing methodology.

EXAMPLE

Figure 10
(Page 2 of 2)

FUNCTIONAL SYSTEM

FLOWCHART NARRATIVE

(1) DATE: May 15, 19XX

(2) SYSTEM NAME: Inventory Status Inquiry Maintenance

(3) PROJECT NO: 7039

(4) PREPARED BY: A. Able

SYSTEM NARRATIVE

MAINTENANCE DEPARTMENT (5)

1. Maintenance employee looks up item number for part which needs to be replaced.

2. The part number is entered on a terminal, and availability and location of the item are requested.

COMPUTER

3. The computer searches the Inventory Master file, locates the item record, and extracts the data needed to answer the inquiry.

MAINTENANCE

4. The data are displayed on the terminal, with an indication of whether or not the part is available, where it is if it is available, and whether or not it is on order if it is not available.

5. If it is available, the Maintenance employee enters a request to reserve the item at the closest storeroom location.

COMPUTER

6. The computer updates the Inventory Master Record with a "demand" against the available balance of the item.

STOREROOM

7. A requisition is printed out on the terminal in the storeroom so that the storeroom personnel can pick the item and have it ready for delivery to Maintenance.

INSTRUCTIONS FOR FORM: PRINTER SPACING CHART

DEFINITION OF EACH ELEMENT:

KEY	ELEMENT/CONTENT
1.	System Name assigned to the system.
2.	Prepared By Name of person preparing the chart.
3.	Date Date the spacing chart was prepared.
4.	Program Number Number of the program which generates the report or document. Should be included on printout if document permits.
5.	Report Title Name of report or document generated.
6.	Heading Identifies the document by name.
7.	Subheadings Identifies columns and other formatted breakdowns.
8.	Notes Include relevant counts, totals, line skips.

Note: X's, 2's, or 9's indicate the total number of characters or numbers that can be printed in each section.

Blank charts are available from computer manufacturers and suppliers.

Figure 11
(Page 2 of 2)

EXAMPLE

PRINTER SPACING CHART

(1) SYSTEM Accounts Receivable (2) PREPARED BY G. Smith (3) DATE 11/8/XX

(4) PROGRAM AR075 (5) REPORT TITLE Accounts Receivable Distribution Report

```
RUN DATE: Z9/99/99            ------------COMPANY NAME PRINTS HERE---------------                        PAGE 999

                   A C C O U N T S   R E C E I V A B L E   D I S T R I B U T I O N   R E P O R T (6)

THRU Z9/99/99 FOR THE PROFIT CENTER:  XXX  XXXXXXXXXXXXXXXXXXXXXXXXXXXXXX

         CASH RECEIPTS SECTION (7)

ACCOUNT   DESCRIPTION                    DATE        AMOUNT
   #

Z999-999  XXXXXXXXXXXXXXXXXXXXXXXXXXXXXX  Z9/99/99  ZZ,ZZZ,ZZZ.99-

                                                                   THIS SECTION HAS SAME FORMAT
                                                                   AS INCOME SECTION.

NEW PAGE
--------------------------------------------------------------------------------------------------------

THRU Z9/99/99 FOR THE PROFIT CENTER: ZZ9

         NET CHANGE TO ACCOUNTS RECEIVALBE                         (8)

ACCOUNT   DESCRIPTION                    DATE        AMOUNT
   #                                                               THIS SECTION HAS SAME FORMAT
                                                                   AS INCOME SECTION, EXCEPT THERE
                                                                   IS NO SECTION TOTAL.
Z999-999  XXXXXXXXXXXXXXXXXXXXXXXXXXXXXX  Z9/99/99  ZZ,ZZZ,ZZZ.99-
```

Figure 12
(Page 1 of 4)

CRT DISPLAY FORMAT

SYSTEM ______ SHEET ___ OF ___ TITLE OF DISPLAY ______

PREPARED BY ______ DATE ______ TASK NUMBER ______

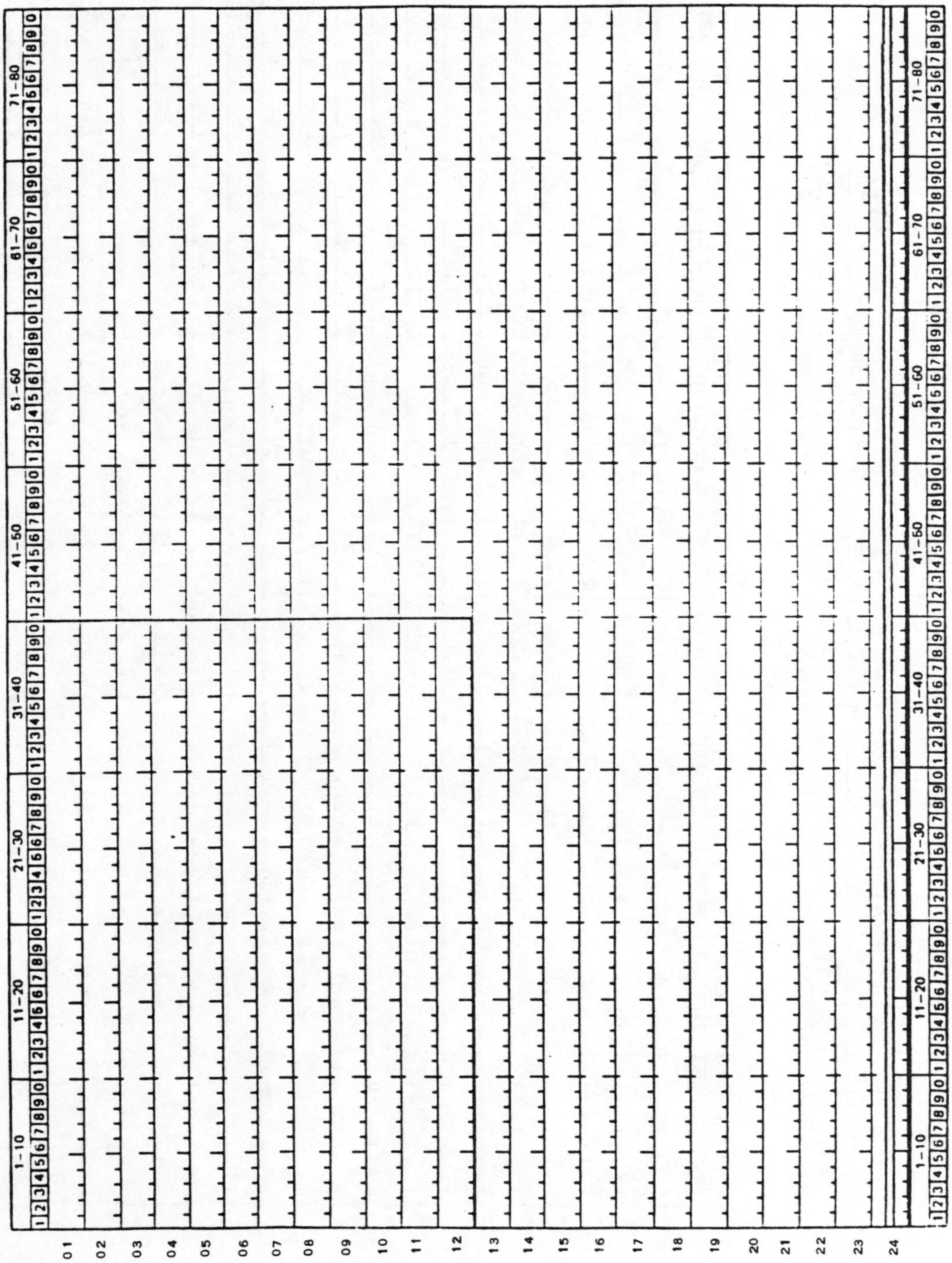

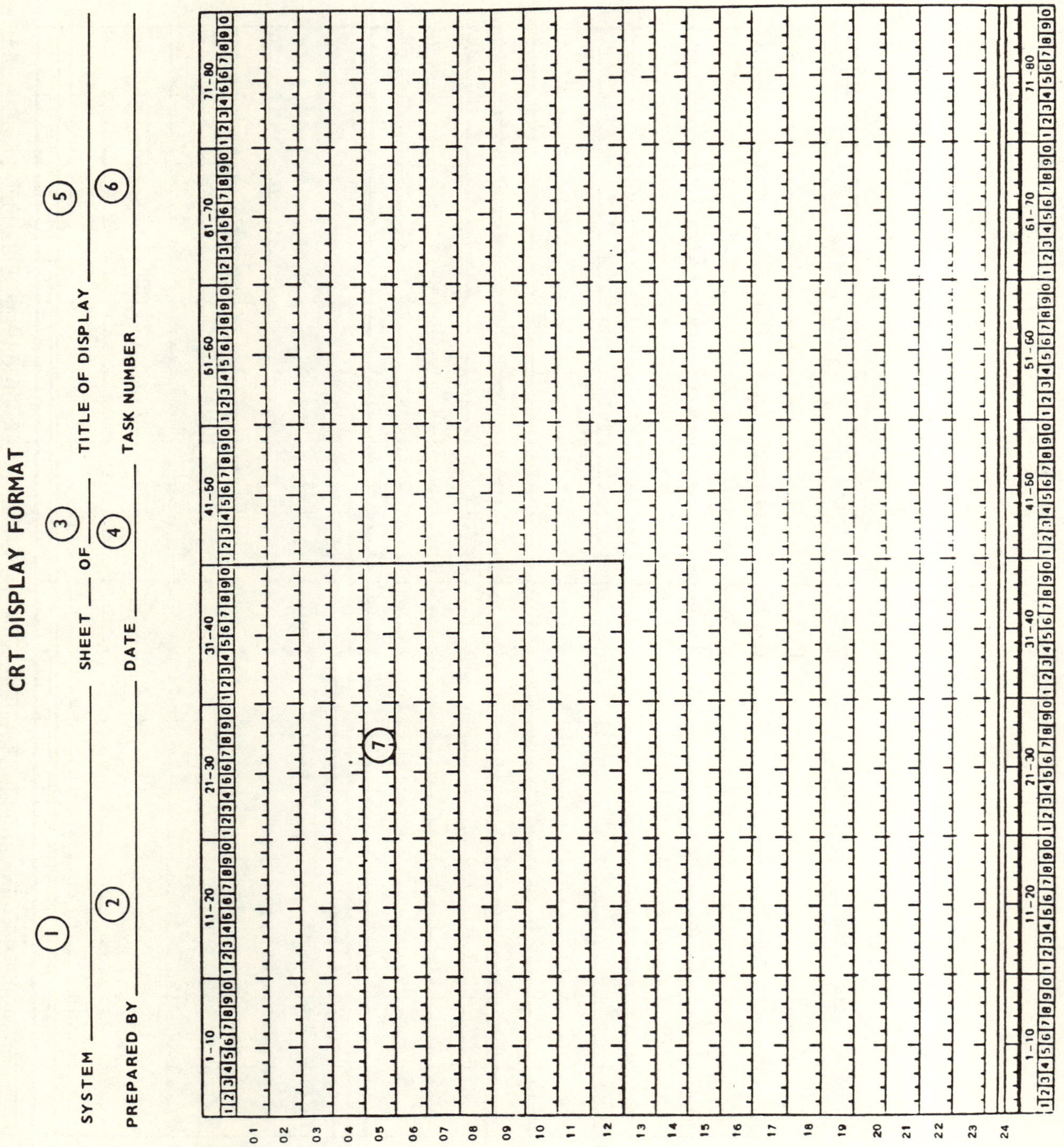
CRT DISPLAY FORMAT
SYSTEM
SHEET
OF
TITLE OF DISPLAY
PREPARED BY
DATE
TASK NUMBER
1-10
11-20
21-30
31-40
41-50
51-60
61-70
71-80

INSTRUCTIONS FOR FORM: CRT DISPLAY FORMAT

DEFINITION OF EACH ELEMENT:

KEY	ELEMENT/CONTENT
1.	System Name assigned to the system.
2.	Prepared By Name of designer of the display.
3.	Sheet Page number and total number of pages used.
4.	Date Date of screen design.
5.	Title of Display Name assigned to the display.
6.	Task Number Task or subtask identifier.
7.	Display Display format as appropriate.

EXAMPLE

Figure 12
(Page 4 of 4)

CRT DISPLAY FORMAT

SYSTEM Supplies Inventory SHEET 1 OF 1 TITLE OF DISPLAY Stores Requisition

PREPARED BY Y. Dutch DATE 8/20/XX TASK NUMBER SISD2Ø

Line	1–80
01	SISD2Ø SUPPLIES INVENTORY
02	
03	STORES REQUISITION NO. ------ CHARGE DEPT NO. ---- ERROR MESSAGE
04	
05	ITEM 1 ID NO. ------- QUANTITY -----
06	2 ------- -----
07	3 ------- -----
08	4 ------- -----
09	5 ------- -----
10	6 ------- -----
11	7 ------- -----
12	8 ------- -----
13	9 ------- -----
14	10 ------- -----
15	11 ------- -----
16	12 ------- -----
17	13 ------- -----
18	14 ------- -----
19	
20	CONTROL TOTAL --------
21	
22	
23	
24	

Figure 13
(Page 1 of 6)

FILE SPECIFICATION RECORD FORMAT

DATE PREPARED ____________

PREPARED BY: ____________

SYSTEM NAME: ____________ PROJECT NO.: ____________

INPUT ☐	FILE NAME ____________	TYPE OF FILE CARD ☐ DISC ☐ MAG. TAPE ☐ DISKETTE ☐ PRINT ☐ ________ ☐	FILE IS USED IN THESE PROGRAMS: ________ ________ ________ ________ ________ ________ ________ ________ ________ ________
OUTPUT ☐	RECORD SIZE ________ FILE NO. ________		
UPDATE ☐	BLOCK SIZE ________ RECORD NO. ________		

FIELD DESCRIPTION	FIELD		FIELD LENGTH IN BYTES	TYPE*	DATA NAME	PICTURE	COMMENTS
	BEG.	END.					

C – character, 8-bit code
X – hexadecimal, 4-bit code B – binary
F – fixed-point, full word
H – fixed-point, halfword
E – floating-point, full word
D – floating-point, double word
P – packed decimal
Z – zoned decimal
A – address value, full word
Y – address value, halfword
V – address, external symbol
S – address, base displacement

Figure 13
(Page 2 of 6)

FILE SPECIFICATION RECORD FORMAT

DATE PREPARED ______ (1)

PREPARED BY: ______ (2)

SYSTEM NAME: ______ (3)   PROJECT NO.: ______ (4)

INPUT ☐ (5) OUTPUT ☐ UPDATE ☐	FILE NAME ______ (6) RECORD SIZE ______ (7) FILE NO. ______ (9) BLOCK SIZE ______ (8) RECORD NO. ______ (10)	TYPE OF FILE (11) CARD ☐ DISC ☐ MAG. TAPE ☐ DISKETTE ☐ PRINT ☐ ______ ☐	FILE IS USED IN THESE PROGRAMS: (12)

FIELD DESCRIPTION	FIELD BEG.	FIELD END.	FIELD LENGTH IN BYTES	TYPE*	DATA NAME	PICTURE	COMMENTS
(13)	(14)		(15)	(16)	(17)	(18)	(19)

C – character, 8-bit code
X – hexadecimal, 4-bit code
B – binary
F – fixed-point, full word
H – fixed-point, halfword
E – floating-point, full word
D – floating-point, double word
P – packed decimal
Z – zoned decimal
A – address value, full word
Y – address value, halfword
V – address, external symbol
S – address, base displacement

INSTRUCTIONS FOR FORM: FILE SPECIFICATION RECORD FORMAT, TYPE 1

DEFINITION OF EACH ELEMENT:

KEY	ELEMENT/CONTENT
1.	Date Prepared Date this sheet is prepared.
2.	Prepared By The person who prepares the specification form.
3.	System Name Name assigned.
4.	Project Number Number assigned to the project.
5.	Input/Output/Update The format being described.
6.	File Name Standard identification name for this file.
7.	Record Size Number of unpacked characters in each record.
8.	Block Size Number of records in each block of data.
9.	File Number Number assigned to the data file.

INSTRUCTIONS FOR FORM: FILE SPECIFICATION RECORD FORMAT, TYPE 1
Continued

DEFINITION OF EACH ELEMENT:

KEY	ELEMENT/CONTENT
10.	Record Number Number assigned to the record.
11.	Type of File Physical media containing the file.
12.	File Is Used in These Programs Identification numbers of the programs using this file.
13.	Field Description Description of each field within the record. Note: List the elements in the order they appear.
14.	Field: Beginning/Ending The starting and ending positions of the field in the file record.
15.	Field Length The number of positions (bytes, characters, etc.) in the field.
16.	Type Type of characters in field. Refer to the key at the bottom of the form.
17.	Data Name Data name used in file description.

INSTRUCTIONS FOR FORM: FILE SPECIFICATION RECORD FORMAT, TYPE 1
Continued

DEFINITION OF EACH ELEMENT:

KEY	ELEMENT/CONTENT
18.	Picture Picture clause used in file description to indicate signs, decimal positions, values, etc.
19.	Comments As deemed appropriate for each field (i.e., "field is optional," "must always contain data").

Figure 13
(Page 6 of 6)

EXAMPLE

FILE SPECIFICATION RECORD FORMAT

DATE PREPARED: 2/17/XX

PREPARED BY: L. Overton

SYSTEM NAME: Hourly Payroll

PROJECT NO.: 892

INPUT ☐ OUTPUT ☐ UPDATE ☐

FILE NAME: Hourly Detail

RECORD SIZE: 50 Bytes FILE NO. 7201

BLOCK SIZE: 2 RECORD NO. 7201.1

TYPE OF FILE: CARD ☐ DISC ☐ MAG. TAPE ☒ DISKETTE ☐ PRINT ☐ Diskette ☐

FILE IS USED IN THESE PROGRAMS:

FIELD DESCRIPTION	FIELD BEG.	FIELD END.	FIELD LENGTH IN BYTES	TYPE*	DATA NAME	PICTURE	COMMENTS
Employee Number	01	08	8	Z	EMPNO	9(5)	File organization: sequential
Employee Name	09	40	32	C	EMPNA	X(20)	
Week Ending Date	41	46	6	Z	WEDATE	99/99/99	
Hours Worked	47	49	3	Z	HRSWKD	99V9	
Shift Designation	50	50	1	Z	SHIFT	9	

C – character, 8-bit code X – hexadecimal, 4-bit code B – binary F – fixed-point, full word H – fixed-point, halfword E – floating-point, full word D – floating-point, double word P – packed decimal Z – zoned decimal A – address value, full word Y – address value, halfword V – address, external symbol S – address, base displacement

Figure 14
(Page 1 of 4)

FILE SPECIFICATION RECORD FORMAT

DATE PREPARED ______________ PREPARED BY: ______________

RECORD LENGTH	BLOCKSIZE	NAME	LABEL	SYSTEM

0	10	20	30	40	50	60	70	80	90
100	110	120	130	140	150	160	170	180	190
200	210	220	230	240	250	260	270	280	290
300	310	320	330	340	350	360	370	380	390
400	410	420	430	440	450	460	470	480	490

FILE SPECIFICATION RECORD FORMAT

DATE PREPARED ______ (1) PREPARED BY: ______ (2)

RECORD LENGTH (3) BLOCKSIZE (4) NAME (5) LABEL (6) SYSTEM (7)

0	10	20	30	40	50	60	70	80	90

(8)

100	110	120	130	140	150	160	170	180	190

200	210	220	230	240	250	260	270	280	290

300	310	320	330	340	350	360	370	380	390

400	410	420	430	440	450	460	470	480	490

INSTRUCTIONS FOR FORM: FILE SPECIFICATION RECORD FORMAT, TYPE 2

DEFINITION OF EACH ELEMENT:

KEY	ELEMENT/CONTENT
1.	Date Prepared The date the record format was prepared.
2.	Prepared By Person who prepared the record format.
3.	Record Length Number of characters in each record.
4.	Blocksize The number of records in each block of data.
5.	Name Name assigned to the record.
6.	Label Standard identification for this record.
7.	System Name assigned
8.	Record Format Identifies specific fields by name and position on the record.

Figure 14
(Page 4 of 4)

EXAMPLE

DATE PREPARED 2/17/XX PREPARED BY: L. OVERTON

FILE SPECIFICATION RECORD FORMAT

RECORD LENGTH 50 BYTES BLOCKSIZE 2 NAME HOURLY DETAIL LABEL HLDT SYSTEM PAYROLL

EMPLOYEE INFORMATION		WEEK ENDING DATE			HRS	SHIFT
NUMBER	NAME	MO	DAY	YR		

0	10	20	30	40	50	60	70	80	90
100	110	120	130	140	150	160	170	180	190
200	210	220	230	240	250	260	270	280	290
300	310	320	330	340	350	360	370	380	390
400	410	420	430	440	450	460	470	480	490

DATA DICTIONARY

DATE ____________________

SYSTEM ____________________ PAGE ______ OF ______

PREPARED BY ____________________ INDEX ____________________

ELEMENT	LABEL	PICTURE	TRANS. REGISTER

DATA DICTIONARY

DATE ③ ____________

SYSTEM ① ____________ PAGE ④ ____ OF ____________

PREPARED BY ② ____________ INDEX ⑤ ____________

ELEMENT	LABEL	PICTURE	TRANS. REGISTER
⑥	⑦	⑧	⑨

INSTRUCTIONS FOR FORM:

DATA DICTIONARY

DEFINITION OF EACH ELEMENT:

KEY	ELEMENT/CONTENT
1.	System Name assigned.
2.	Prepared By The person who prepared the data dictionary.
3.	Date Date the dictionary was prepared.
4.	Page Page number and total number of pages.
5.	Index The first letter of the data elements recorded on this page. (A separate page is set up for each letter of the alphabet for larger dictionaries.)
6.	Element Descriptive name for this data element.
7.	Label The standard label to be used for this data element in all programs and documentation.

INSTRUCTIONS FOR FORM: DATA DICTIONARY--Continued

DEFINITION OF EACH ELEMENT:

KEY	ELEMENT/CONTENT
8.	Picture Description of the element as it is used in programs, for example, S9(5)V99.
9.	Transaction Register If displayed on variable-format transaction registers, this is the code identifying this data element.

EXAMPLE

DATA DICTIONARY

DATE 8/4/XX

SYSTEM Supplies Inventory

PAGE 1 OF 1

PREPARED BY Y. Dutch

INDEX

ELEMENT	LABEL	PICTURE	TRANS. REGISTER
Account Number	Account	9(4)	
Description of Supply Item	Descr	X(3Ø)	
Issued to Date (Quantity)	Iss-to-Date	S9(7)	
Item-ID (Supply Item)	Item-ID	X(6)	
Order Point (Reorder)	Order-PT	S9(7)	
Order Quantity	Order-Q	S9(7)	
Price (Issue U/M)	Price	S9(5)V99	
Quantity on Hand	On-Hand	S9(7)	
Quantity on Order	On-Order	S9(7)	
Quantity Order to Date	Ord-to-Date	S9(7)	
Unit of Measure-Issue	Unit-Issue	X(8)	
Unit of Measure-Purchase	Unit-Pch	X(8)	
Vendors	Vendors	X(25)	

Figure 16
(Page 1 of 4)

EDITING RULES

PAGE ________ OF ________

SYSTEM: ______________________ PREPARED BY: ______________________

INPUT: ______________________ DATE PREPARED: ______________________

DATA ELEMENT	OPT/REQ.	A/N	EDITS

Figure 16
(Page 2 of 4)

EDITING RULES

SYSTEM: (1) ____________________ PAGE (3) ______ OF ______

INPUT: (2) ____________________ PREPARED BY: (4) ____________________

DATE PREPARED: (5) ____________________

DATA ELEMENT	OPT/REQ.	A/N	EDITS
(6)	(7)	(8)	(9)

INSTRUCTIONS FOR FORM:

EDITING RULES

DEFINITION OF EACH ELEMENT:

KEY	ELEMENT/CONTENT
1.	System Name assigned to the system.
2.	Input Name of data record or display to be edited.
3.	Page Indicate the page number and the total number of pages.
4.	Prepared By Name of preparer.
5.	Date Date of preparation.
6.	Data Element Descriptive name of this data element.
7.	Opt/Req Indication whether data element is optional or required.
8.	A/N Designation of the element to be edited specifically as alphabetic (A), numeric (N), or alphanumeric (A/N).
9.	Edits Other specific edit tests--including relationship edits--which must be performed on this data element.

Figure 16
(Page 4 of 4)

EXAMPLE

EDITING RULES

PAGE 1 OF 1

SYSTEM: Stores Requisition

PREPARED BY: G. Jones

INPUT: SISD2ØI

DATE PREPARED: 4/15/XX

DATA ELEMENT	OPT/REQ.	A/N	EDITS
Requisition No.	R	N	
Department No.	R	N	
Items:			
Item ID No.	R	A/N	Must be on SIS Data Base
Quantity	R	N	Required for any line with ITEM ID NO.

Note: Must be at least one ITEM ID NO.--QUANTITY LINE. May be only one such line or any number up to a full screen (12).

Figure 17
(Page 1 of 4)

ELEMENT VALUE TABLE

SYSTEM: ______________________________ PREPARED BY: ____________________

TITLE: ______________________________ DATE PREPARED: ____________________

LABEL: ______________ PICTURE: ______________

VALUE	DESCRIPTION

ELEMENT VALUE TABLE

SYSTEM: ① ____________________

TITLE: ② ____________________

LABEL: ③ __________ PICTURE: ④ __________

PREPARED BY: ⑤ ____________________

DATE PREPARED: ⑥ ____________________

VALUE	DESCRIPTION
⑦	⑧

INSTRUCTIONS FOR FORM:

ELEMENT VALUE TABLE

DEFINITION OF EACH ELEMENT:

KEY	ELEMENT/CONTENT
1.	System Name of system to which this element is applicable.
2.	Title Descriptive name for this data element.
3.	Label The standard label to be used for this element in all programs and documentation.
4.	Picture Description of the element as it is used in programs, for example, S9(5)V99.
5.	Prepared By Name of preparer.
6.	Date Prepared Date of preparation.
7.	Value The valid values for this item are recorded in this column.
8.	Description The meaning of the corresponding value for this element.

EXAMPLE

ELEMENT VALUE TABLE

SYSTEM: Supplies Inventory

PREPARED BY: Y. Dutch

TITLE: Item Status Code

DATE PREPARED: 8/15/XX

LABEL: Status PICTURE: X

VALUE	DESCRIPTION
A	Active Item
D	Pending Deletion--No Further Activity Permitted

EXAMPLE

Figure 18

DATA CONTROL CONCEPTS

Data controls are incorporated in the system at two levels. At data entry, a hash total of quantities for each purchase order, receiving document, and stores requisition is entered, and the data are verified before they are accepted and the data base is updated.

Processing controls consisting of counts of "active" and "pending deletion" records on the data base are taken with each backup and restore run performed.

Month-to-date transaction file record counts are taken and printed each time the merging of daily files into the month-to-date file is performed.

DATA SECURITY CONCEPTS

Access to data base update functions is restricted to the terminal located in the central supplies storeroom. Access will be further restricted by use of a common password to be used by all authorized storeroom personnel. This password will be changed on a regular basis and, in addition, each time there is a change in storeroom personnel.

OPERATING ENVIRONMENT IMPACT STATEMENT

The on-line demands of this application are minimal. Anticipated transaction volumes will account for an increase of approximately 200 transactions daily compared to the existing transaction volume of over 14,000 transactions for all other applications. There are no unique hardware requirements considered for this system.

DOCUMENT ANALYSIS SHEET

DATE PREPARED: ____________________

SYSTEM NAME: ____________________

SYSTEM NO.: ____________________ PREPARED BY: ____________________

DOCUMENT:		
FORM NUMBER:	SIZE:	NO. OF PARTS
PURPOSE:		

DISTRIBUTION:

FORM PART & COLOR	DEPT.	USE BY RECIPIENT

	CYCLE	AVERAGE	PEAK	PROJECTED
VOLUME AND CYCLE:				

NUMBER OF LINES PER DOCUMENT:

AVERAGE NUMBER OF CHARACTERS PER LINE:

PREPARED BY:

SOURCE OF INFORMATION:

METHOD OF PREPARATION:

PREPARATION TIME:

COMMENTS:

ATTACH FILLED-IN SAMPLE

DOCUMENT ANALYSIS SHEET

DATE PREPARED: (1) ______________

SYSTEM NAME: (2) ______________

SYSTEM NO.: (3) ______________ PREPARED BY: (4) ______________

DOCUMENT: (5)		
FORM NUMBER: (6)	SIZE: (7)	NO. OF PARTS (8)
PURPOSE: (9)		

DISTRIBUTION:

FORM PART & COLOR (10)	DEPT. (11)	USE BY RECIPIENT (12)

	CYCLE	AVERAGE	PEAK	PROJECTED
VOLUME AND CYCLE:	(13)	(14)	(15)	(16)

NUMBER OF LINES PER DOCUMENT:	(17)
AVERAGE NUMBER OF CHARACTERS PER LINE:	(18)
PREPARED BY:	(19)
SOURCE OF INFORMATION:	(20)
METHOD OF PREPARATION:	(21)
PREPARATION TIME:	(22)
COMMENTS:	(23)

(24) ATTACH FILLED-IN SAMPLE

INSTRUCTIONS FOR FORM: DOCUMENT ANALYSIS SHEET

DEFINITION OF EACH ELEMENT:

KEY	ELEMENT/CONTENT
1.	Date Prepared The date this sheet was prepared.
2.	System Name Name assigned to the system.
3.	System Number Number assigned to the system.
4.	Prepared By The person who prepared the document.
5.	Document Title of the form being analyzed.
6.	Form Number The number used to identify the form.
7.	Size Physical dimensions, e.g., 5" X 7".
8.	Number of Parts Number of parts or pages to the document.
9.	Purpose Primary purpose for which the form is used.

INSTRUCTIONS FOR FORM: DOCUMENT ANALYSIS SHEET--Continued

DEFINITION OF EACH ELEMENT:

KEY	ELEMENT/CONTENT
10.	Form Part and Color Form part number and its color. Account for total number of parts as shown in item 8. Use another sheet if there are more than four parts.
11.	Department Department or area which receives this part of the form set.
12.	Use by Recipient Specific use(s) by this department.
13.	Cycle Processing cycles for form.
14.	Average Average number of documents prepared in each cycle.
15.	Peak Peak number of documents prepared per cycle.
16.	Projected Projected average number of documents prepared one year from today.
17.	Number of Lines per Document Average number of data lines including heading data lines on the document.

INSTRUCTIONS FOR FORM: DOCUMENT ANALYSIS SHEET--Continued

DEFINITION OF EACH ELEMENT:

KEY	ELEMENT/CONTENT
18.	Average Characters per Line Average number of data characters per line.
19.	Prepared By Department name and job title of person who originates this form.
20.	Source of Information Source document of the information filled in.
21.	Method of Preparation Manual, typed, data entry, etc.
22.	Preparation Time Time required to fill in one form, usually shown in minutes.
23.	Comments Strengths of form according to users and analyst, and suggested ways to improve the value of the form.
24.	Attachment Attach a filled-in sample of the form.

Note: The document analysis sheet is to be used to describe both input documents and output reports used in existing and proposed systems.

EXAMPLE

DOCUMENT ANALYSIS SHEET

DATE PREPARED: 2/14/XX

SYSTEM NAME: Simplify Purchase Handling

SYSTEM NO.: 7050 PREPARED BY: D. Ramlow

DOCUMENT:	Purchase Order		
FORM NUMBER:	X419	SIZE: 5 x 7	NO. OF PARTS 4
PURPOSE:	Place order with vendor		

DISTRIBUTION:

FORM PART & COLOR	DEPT.	USE BY RECIPIENT
1 White	Vendor	Process our order
2 White	Purchasing	Follow-up
3 Yellow	Requester	Notice that order is placed and follow up
4 Green	Receiving	Match with incoming goods

	CYCLE	AVERAGE	PEAK	PROJECTED
VOLUME AND CYCLE:	Daily	20	30	25

NUMBER OF LINES PER DOCUMENT: 5

AVERAGE NUMBER OF CHARACTERS PER LINE: 20

PREPARED BY:	Purchasing clerk
SOURCE OF INFORMATION:	Purchase requisition (4 x 7)
METHOD OF PREPARATION:	Typed
PREPARATION TIME:	15 Minutes

COMMENTS: Form is easy to learn and simple to file and find, but is poorly zoned, uses old type styles, and produces illegible copies unless the typist uses an electric typewriter.

ATTACH FILLED-IN SAMPLE

Figure 20
(Page 1 of 4)

GLOSSARY OF SYSTEMS TERMS

DATE PREPARED: ______________________

PREPARED BY: ______________________

SYSTEM NAME: ______________________ SYSTEM NO.: ______________________

TERM	DATA NAME	DEFINITION	CODES	MEANING OF CODES

Figure 20
(Page 2 of 4)

GLOSSARY OF SYSTEMS TERMS

(1)

DATE PREPARED: ______ (2)

PREPARED BY: ______ (4)

SYSTEM NAME: ______ (3)

SYSTEM NO.: ______

TERM	DATA NAME	DEFINITION	CODES	MEANING OF CODES
(5)	(6)	(7)	(8)	(9)

INSTRUCTIONS FOR FORM: GLOSSARY OF SYSTEMS TERMS

DEFINITION OF EACH ELEMENT:

KEY	ELEMENT/CONTENT
1.	Date Prepared The date the glossary of systems terms was prepared.
2.	Prepared By Person who prepared the Glossary of Systems Terms.
3.	System Name Name assigned to the system or project.
4.	System Number Number assigned to the system or project.
5.	Term The item being described and defined.
6.	Data Name Specifies the label used in computer programs. This element is added to the glossary during computer system development.
7.	Definition Specifies the meaning of the term as used in this system.
8.	Codes Identifies alphabetic or numeric codes associated with each term. Usually added to the glossary during system development.
9.	Meaning of Codes Specifies the meaning of each code associated with a term.

Figure 20
(Page 4 of 4)

EXAMPLE

GLOSSARY OF SYSTEMS TERMS

DATE PREPARED: 3/25/XX

PREPARED BY: B. Baker

SYSTEM NAME: Payroll Reporting

SYSTEM NO.: 7050

TERM	DATA NAME	DEFINITION	CODES	MEANING OF CODES
Tax Exemption	TAXFED	Exemption in dollars allowed in tax calculations	1	Federal Exemption
	TAXST		2	State Exemption
	TAXLC		3	Local Exemption

INSTRUCTIONS FOR FORM: LETTER OF INTENT

DEFINITION OF EACH ELEMENT:

KEY	ELEMENT/CONTENT
1.	Vendor Address of vendor.
2.	Equipment List each requested component with its full model number and name. Include any other relevant factors, such as core size.
3.	Monthly Rental Include the monthly rental charge as supplied by the vendor's representative. Indicate items supplied without charge.
4.	Delivery Date Specify the required delivery date.
5.	Installation Specify the date by which installation must be completed.
6.	Option to Cancel Declare an option to cancel the order up to a specified date.
7.	Site Planner Request the services of a site planning engineer to advise on the physical requirements of installation enumerated in item 8.

INSTRUCTIONS FOR FORM:

LETTER OF INTENT--Continued

DEFINITION OF EACH ELEMENT:

KEY	ELEMENT/CONTENT
8.	Checklist

Request information in writing on all aspects of installation, such as the requirements in these areas:

Layouts.
Floor weight--load.
Electrical.
Safety voltage to prevent loss of data.
Room temperature and humidity.
Free test time.
Computer training.
Maintenance and service charges.

Note: The letter is free-form, but must contain the above-mentioned points.

XYZ corporation

EXAMPLE

(1)

J. Smith, Sales Representative
ABC Computer Company
12345 Walnut Street
Tulsa, Oklahoma

Dear Mr. Smith:

It is our intent to place an order for the following ABC System 2002/Model 97 Equipment:

Equipment (2)	Monthly Rental (3)
Main Storage (8,192 Bytes) 4029 Processing Unit, Model C14	$ 720
2501 Disk Storage, Model 2 (40 MB)	490
2520 Diskette Drive, Model A3	283
2403 Printer, Model 16, and attachments, 1100 lines per minute	1,283
	$2,776

(4)

The required delivery date is December 1, 19XX. The required date for completion of installation is December 31, 19XX. (5)

(6)

We maintain the option of canceling this order until September 1, 19XX.

Please supply us with a Site Planning Engineer by July 15, 19XX to help determine the following: (7)

1. Floor layout requirements. (8)

2. Floor weight-load demands.

3. Electrical requirements.

4. The lowest the voltage can drop without causing loss of data.

5. Air temperature and humidity requirements.

In a separate letter, will you please specify the following:

1. Amount of free testing hours at the ABC Test Center.

2. Maintenance and service charges.

3. Recommended and required software.

4. Recommended computer classes and programmed instruction courses.

Sincerely,

A. Larson
Manager of Computer
Services

Figure 22
(Page 1 of 5)

PROGRESS REPORT

DATE PREPARED: ____________________

SYSTEM NAME: ____________________

SYSTEM NO.: ____________________ PREPARED BY: ____________________

CATEGORY	ORIGINAL ESTIMATE	CURRENT ESTIMATE	EXPENDITURE TO DATE	PERCENT TO ORIGINAL ESTIMATE	PERCENT TO CURRENT ESTIMATE
I. PROJECT STATUS					
Date Project Started					
Completion Target					
Total Dollars to Install:					
System & Programming					
User					
Clerical					
Outside Services					
Computer Time					
Travel					
Meetings					
Supplies					
Staffing					
Training					
Contingency					
Total Man-Weeks to Install					
User Management					
User Personnel					
Systems Management					
Analysts					
DP Operations Personnel					
	SCHEDULED NUMBER	PERCENT SCHEDULED	ACTUAL NUMBER	PERCENT ACTUAL	
II. CURRENT PROGRESS					
Tasks Started					
Tasks Completed					
Tasks Outstanding					

Use Additional Pages to Report Key Events and Recommendations

Figure 22
(Page 2 of 5)

PROGRESS REPORT

(1)
DATE PREPARED: ______________________

(2)
SYSTEM NAME: ______________________

(3)
SYSTEM NO.: ______________________ (4) PREPARED BY: ______________________

CATEGORY	ORIGINAL ESTIMATE	CURRENT ESTIMATE	EXPENDITURE TO DATE	PERCENT TO ORIGINAL ESTIMATE	PERCENT TO CURRENT ESTIMATE
I. PROJECT STATUS (5)					
Date Project Started					
Completion Target					
Total Dollars to Install:					
System & Programming					
User					
Clerical					
Outside Services					
Computer Time					
Travel					
Meetings					
Supplies					
Staffing					
Training					
Contingency					
Total Man-Weeks to Install					
User Management					
User Personnel					
Systems Management					
Analysts					
DP Operations Personnel					
	SCHEDULED NUMBER	PERCENT SCHEDULED	ACTUAL NUMBER	PERCENT ACTUAL	
II. CURRENT PROGRESS (6)					
Tasks Started					
Tasks Completed					
Tasks Outstanding					

(7) & (8)

Use Additional Pages to Report Key Events and Recommendations

INSTRUCTIONS FOR FORM: PROGRESS REPORT

DEFINITION OF EACH ELEMENT:

KEY **ELEMENT/CONTENT**

1. Date Prepared

   Date the Progress Report was prepared.

2. System Name

   Name assigned to the system.

3. System Number

   Number assigned to the system.

4. Prepared By

   Analyst who prepared the Progress Report.

5. Project Status

   The current status of the project. The detailed items of project status (start date, completion date, cost categories, and time to install) are reported in terms of (a) the original estimate, (b) a current estimate, (c) the expenditure to date, (d) percentage of expenditure to original estimate, and (e) percentage of expenditure to current estimate.

6. Current Progress

   The percentage of actual task completion to the number of task completions scheduled. Tasks started, completed, and outstanding are reported in terms of (a) scheduled progress to date (number of tasks scheduled for completion, as well as percentage of tasks scheduled for completion to total tasks scheduled) and (b) actual progress to date (absolute number as well as percentage of tasks actually completed to total tasks scheduled).

Note: The following items are reported in narrative format.

7. General Summary

Key events which have taken place since last progress report are presented in narrative form. This section is used to interpret the meaning of the figures and percentages reported in earlier sections.

8. Recommendations

Current and anticipated problems are reported together with recommended solutions. Examples might include project slippage, nonparticipation of key personnel, equipment delays, and unresolved management decisions.

EXAMPLE

Figure 22
(Page 5 of 5)

PROGRESS REPORT

DATE PREPARED: 3/24/XX

SYSTEM NAME: Inventory

SYSTEM NO.: 197 PREPARED BY: P. Jones

CATEGORY	ORIGINAL ESTIMATE	CURRENT ESTIMATE	EXPENDITURE TO DATE	PERCENT TO ORIGINAL ESTIMATE	PERCENT TO CURRENT ESTIMATE
I. PROJECT STATUS					
Date Project Started	1/12/XX	-	-	-	-
Completion Target	4/30/XX	5/15/XX	-	-	-
Total Dollars to Install:	50,000	60,000	30,000	60%	50%
System & Programming	20,000	25,000	20,000	100%	80%
User	5,000	5,000	2,000	40%	40%
Clerical	1,000	1,000	-	-	-
Outside Services	-	1,000	-	-	-
Computer Time	8,000	10,000	2,000	25%	20%
Travel	2,000	1,000	-	-	-
Meetings	2,000	3,000	2,000	100%	66%
Supplies	3,000	5,000	3,000	100%	60%
Staffing	1,000	1,000	500	50%	50%
Training	1,000	1,000	500	50%	50%
Contingency	7,000	7,000	-	-	-
Total Man-Weeks to Install	27	37	19	70%	51%
User Management	1	1	1	100%	100%
User Personnel	3	6	2	66%	33%
Systems Management	1	1	-	-	-
Analysts	20	25	15	75%	60%
DP Operations Personnel	2	4	1	50%	25%
	SCHEDULED NUMBER	PERCENT SCHEDULED	ACTUAL NUMBER	PERCENT ACTUAL	
II. CURRENT PROGRESS					
Tasks Started	100	48%	75	30%	
Tasks Completed	50	24%	25	10%	
Tasks Outstanding	60	28%	0	80%	

Use Additional Pages to Report Key Events and Recommendations

Figure 23
(Page 1 of 4)

LIST OF REQUIRED CLERICAL DESK INSTRUCTIONS

DATE PREPARED: ____________________

SYSTEM NAME: ____________________

SYSTEM NO.: ____________________ PREPARED BY: ____________________

NUMBER	TITLE OF CLERICAL DESK INSTRUCTION	DESCRIPTION

LIST OF REQUIRED CLERICAL DESK INSTRUCTIONS

DATE PREPARED: ______ (1)

SYSTEM NAME: ______ (2)

SYSTEM NO.: ______ (3) PREPARED BY: ______ (4)

NUMBER	TITLE OF CLERICAL DESK INSTRUCTION	DESCRIPTION
(5)	(6)	(7)

INSTRUCTIONS FOR FORM:

LIST OF REQUIRED CLERICAL
DESK INSTRUCTIONS

DEFINITION OF EACH ELEMENT:

KEY	ELEMENT/CONTENT
1.	Date Prepared Date this sheet is prepared.
2.	System Name Name assigned to the system.
3.	System Number Number assigned to the system.
4.	Prepared By Analyst who prepared the list.
5.	Clerical Desk Instruction Number The number assigned to the desk instruction.
6.	Title of Desk Instruction The name assigned to the desk instruction.
7.	Description Brief description, in general terms, of the clerical job that must be performed.

EXAMPLE

LIST OF REQUIRED CLERICAL DESK INSTRUCTIONS

DATE PREPARED: 4/21/XX

SYSTEM NAME: Payroll

SYSTEM NO.: 2001 PREPARED BY: G. Zoldi

NUMBER	TITLE OF CLERICAL DESK INSTRUCTION	DESCRIPTION
P-106	Balancing Payroll Input Data	The instructions for developing the control totals which computer operations will balance in order to ensure that all transactions have been processed.
P-204	Payroll Error Corrections	The instructions for correcting errors that were made in an employee's paycheck.

JOB DESCRIPTION

DATE PREPARED: ____________________

SYSTEM NAME: ____________________

SYSTEM NO.: ____________________ PREPARED BY: ____________________

JOB TITLE:
DIVISION:
DEPARTMENT:
LOCATION:

GRADE

FUNCTION:

RELATIONSHIP:

DUTIES:

Figure 24
(Page 2 of 5)

JOB DESCRIPTION

DATE PREPARED: ______ (1)

SYSTEM NAME: ______ (2)

SYSTEM NO.: ______ (3) PREPARED BY: ______ (4)

JOB TITLE: (5)
DIVISION: (7)
DEPARTMENT: (8)
LOCATION: (9)

GRADE (6)

FUNCTION: (10)

RELATIONSHIP: (11)

DUTIES: (12)

INSTRUCTIONS FOR FORM: JOB DESCRIPTION

DEFINITION OF EACH ELEMENT:

KEY	ELEMENT/CONTENT
1.	Date Prepared Date the job description was prepared.
2.	System Name Name assigned to system.
3.	System Number Number assigned to system.
4.	Prepared By Analyst who prepared the job description.
5.	Job Title Title of the position being described.
6.	Grade Level of the position being described.
7.	Division Division in which the position being described is located.

INSTRUCTIONS FOR FORM: JOB DESCRIPTION--Continued

DEFINITION OF EACH ELEMENT:

KEY	ELEMENT/CONTENT
8.	Department Department within division in which position is located.
9.	Location Geographic location of the position being described.
10.	Function Concise statement of basic purpose of position.
11.	Relationship Position to which the position being described reports.
12.	Duties List, in sequence of relative importance, of the major duties of the position described.

EXAMPLE

JOB DESCRIPTION

DATE PREPARED: 3/11/XX

SYSTEM NAME: Training Records

SYSTEM NO.: 117 PREPARED BY: I. Sarnat

JOB TITLE: Educational Assistant **GRADE** T-2
DIVISION: Computer and Systems Services
DEPARTMENT: Financial Services
LOCATION: New York

FUNCTION: Plans and coordinates the training of technical employees in the Computer and Systems Services Department.

RELATIONSHIP: Responsible to Vice President of Computer and Systems Services Department.

DUTIES:

1. Implements and re-evaluates educational plan

   a. Maintains study material
   b. Establishes training sequence for each student
   c. Prepares student's training schedule
   d. Conducts classes as determined by Educational Coordinator.
   e. Develops visuals, course outlines, other training materials.

2. Assists Vice President in evaluating performance of trainees.

   a. Maintains necessary records for each student.

3. Keeps technically informed on latest developments in the systems field, computer industry, and teaching techniques.

INSTRUCTIONS FOR FORM:

SYSTEM TEST PLAN

DEFINITION OF EACH ELEMENT:

KEY	ELEMENT/CONTENT
1.	Scope The extent to which the system will be tested during the systems test phase. The scope must be further detailed into: a. How long each cycle of testing will take. b. Which organizational units at various locations will participate in the systems test. c. Data to be inputted and the volume of data to be tested.
2.	Approach The manner in which the systems test will be conducted. This must be further detailed into: a. How the data will be prepared. b. What files will be required and how they will be created. c. How the results will be analyzed for acceptability. d. Criteria to be used to measure the system in light of management objectives and performance criteria. e. What methods will be used for making changes to correct errors. f. Plans of action if the system does not meet the criteria. g. Whether the test will include a volume test or parallel test.

INSTRUCTIONS FOR FORM: SYSTEM TEST PLAN--Continued

DEFINITION OF EACH ELEMENT:

KEY	ELEMENT/CONTENT
3.	Responsibilities

Responsibilities for the activities conducted during the system's test phase, such as:

a. Who will train the users for preparing the data.

b. Who will prepare the data.

c. Who will schedule the tests.

d. Who will generate the files required.

e. Who will evaluate the results.

f. Who will determine what changes are to be made.

g. Who will decide whether the systems test was a success or failure.

h. Who will ensure that all operating instructions are current and accurate.

i. Who will determine that the system is operational.

EXAMPLE

SYSTEM TEST PLAN

PAYROLL/PERSONNEL PROJECT 420

DATE PREPARED: 01/02/XX

PREPARED BY: R. Neuf

(1.) SCOPE

The system test for the Personnel/Payroll Masterfile System will be divided into four (4) major areas:

A. Conversion

B. Masterfile Updating

C. Payroll (checks and reports)

D. Personnel Reports

Length of testing

A. Conversion: 3 or more conversions of tape records to a new disk file until level of missing data is below 2%.

3 or more computer edits of converted data until validity level is above 97%.

1 or more computer print-outs distributed to employees for review and error correction.

B. Masterfile Updating: 1 month of successful, daily masterfile updating via terminal and 1 month of successful daily masterfile updating via batch program.

C. Payroll:

1. Checks - two months (4 semimonthly payroll runs) of parallel runs.

2. Reports - 2 semimonthly payroll runs of deduction reports.

1 run of government reports consisting of figures from 4 parallel payroll runs.

D. Personnel: 1 run per report (all frequencies) at the end of the second parallel payroll run.

EXAMPLE

Types of data to be tested

A. All programs will be tested using a selected file of approximately 200 employee records.

B. Payroll parallels will consist of about 500 employees selected by division, department, etc., to be representative of most conditions.

C. Payroll parallels will consist of all employees after successful runs using 500 employees.

D. Personnel reports will be tested using 200 employee records and then all employees.

(2.) APPROACH

1. Initial data will be created by converting test card files and production files.

2. Masterfile updating will consist of actual production transactions applied via video terminal.

3. Payroll parallels will consist of actual salaries and time cards where applicable.

4. Payroll internal reports will be checked to figures from parallel runs.

5. Payroll government reports will be checked for validity and reasonableness. No parallel is possible.

6. Personnel reports will be checked for validity, reasonableness, and cross-checked to existing mechanized and manual reports where possible.

7. Terminal updating response time must be within 5 seconds.

(3.) RESPONSIBILITIES

The following units will participate in the systems test:

1. Payroll

   A. Verify the accuracy of all checks

   B. Verify the accuracy of internal payroll reports

EXAMPLE

C. Validate the contents of government reports

D. Prepare all necessary payroll data for payroll parallel runs

E. Evaluate operational end of printer terminal

2. Personnel

   A. Validate all personnel reports

   B. Prepare all nonpayroll transactions for video terminal updating

   C. Evaluate operational end of video terminals

   D. Determine when system is operational and ready for installation

3. Data Control

   A. Assist in all report check-out

   B. Determine that all controls have been developed and are functioning

4. Project Development

   A. Train users for data preparation

   B. Train users for video and printer terminal operation

   C. Evaluate terminal operation and response

   D. Schedule all tests

   E. Revise all programs and procedures as required by test

INSTRUCTIONS FOR FORM: USER TRAINING PLAN

DEFINITION OF EACH ELEMENT:

KEY	ELEMENT/CONTENT
1.	Type of Training The type of training to be undertaken. Training should be identified in terms of: Lectures Class discussions Sample problems Tests "Hands-on" experience (for new equipment)
2.	Who Will Receive Training The level of management receiving the training. Also identify organization units involved in the training program.
3.	Training Curriculum The subject matter to be presented during the training program.
4.	Who Will Conduct the Training The personnel who will conduct the training. Specific reference must be made to: User personnel Vendor personnel Systems personnel
5.	When and Where Will the Training be Conducted The duration of the training, the scheduled calendar dates, the time of day, and at what locations the training will take place.

EXAMPLE

Figure 26
(Page 2 of 3)

USER TRAINING PLAN

PAYROLL/PERSONNEL PROJECT 420

DATE PREPARED: 01/02/XX

PREPARED BY: R. Meuf

(1.) TYPE OF TRAINING

Training for all users involved will consist of lectures, class discussions, hands-on experience where new equipment is involved, and sample problems.

(2.) WHO WILL RECEIVE TRAINING

The training program will involve the following people:

1. Manager of Employee Compensation
2. Manager of Personnel
3. Payroll Supervisor
4. Four clerical input coders and terminal operators
5. Data Control Supervisor
6. Company supervisors

(3.) TRAINING CURRICULUM

1. Philosophy and objectives of new system
2. Use of new forms in the system
3. Use and understanding of new coding
4. Familiarization with documentation and procedure manual
5. Mechanical operation of video and typewriter terminals
6. System use of terminals (hands-on problems)
7. Use of exception time reporting

EXAMPLE

Figure 26
(Page 3 of 3)

(4.) WHO WILL CONDUCT THE TRAINING

1. The project leader will supervise the overall training with the assistance of team members.

2. An equipment representative will teach the mechanical operation of the video and typewriter terminals.

3. A bulletin, procedure write-up, and sample problems will instruct Company supervisors on the use of exception time reporting under control of the Manager of Employee Compensation.

(5.) WHEN AND WHERE WILL TRAINING BE CONDUCTED

1. Exception time reporting: Month of June 19XX.

2. User systems presentation and terminal training:

   May 17-28, 1:00 P.M. - 3:00 P.M., Personnel Department conference room and computer room.

Figure 27
(Page 1 of 5)

SYSTEM TEST DATA

DATE PREPARED: ____________________

SYSTEM NAME: ____________________

SYSTEM NO.: ____________________ PREPARED BY: ____________________

ITEM NO.	DESCRIPTION	MEDIA	REFERENCE DOCUMENT	LOCATION

ANTICIPATED TEST RESULTS

SYSTEM TEST DATA

(1)
DATE PREPARED: ______

(2)
SYSTEM NAME: ______

(3) (4)
SYSTEM NO.: ______ PREPARED BY: ______

ITEM NO.	DESCRIPTION	MEDIA	REFERENCE DOCUMENT	LOCATION
(5)	(6)	(7)	(8)	(9)

ANTICIPATED TEST RESULTS

(10)

INSTRUCTIONS FOR FORM: SYSTEM TEST DATA

DEFINITION OF EACH ELEMENT:

KEY	ELEMENT/CONTENT
1.	Date Prepared The date when the test data were prepared.
2.	System Name Name assigned to the system.
3.	System Number Number assigned to the system.
4.	Prepared By The analyst who prepared the system test data.
5.	Item Number Sequential number assigned to all system inputs.
6.	Description Brief description of system input, e.g., payment, customer order, master file.
7.	Media Physical form of the input, e.g., disk, tape.

INSTRUCTIONS FOR FORM: SYSTEM TEST DATA--Continued

DEFINITION OF EACH ELEMENT:

KEY	ELEMENT/CONTENT
8.	Reference Document If input is created from another document, list that document here.
9.	Location Physical location of input test media.
10.	Anticipated Test Results Narrative description of expected results of systems test.

EXAMPLE

SYSTEM TEST DATA

DATE PREPARED: 3/2/XX

SYSTEM NAME: Payroll/Personnel

SYSTEM NO.: 20-307-2 PREPARED BY: A. Huber

ITEM NO.	DESCRIPTION	MEDIA	REFERENCE DOCUMENT	LOCATION
1	Salary Changes	Disk	Listing	DP Operation
2	Employer Master File	Tape		

ANTICIPATED TEST RESULTS

System should produce updated listing of all employees by department, indicating gross annual salary, last raise, and net biweekly pay.

Figure 28

INSTRUCTIONS FOR FORM: SYSTEM TEST RESULTS

DEFINITION OF EACH ELEMENT:

KEY **ELEMENT/CONTENT**

Since this information takes a varying form with each system, no specific form is provided. The documents include the actual output of the systems test. They are used to evaluate testing against the systems test plan.

INSTRUCTIONS FOR FORM: INSTALLATION PLAN

DEFINITION OF EACH ELEMENT:

KEY	ELEMENT/CONTENT
1.	Scope

The manner in which the system will be installed. This section should indicate whether installation of the system shall be:

On a pilot basis.

On a parallel basis.

Partial (a portion of the system).

Full (entire system throughout the company).

2. Approach

The manner in which the installation of the system will be conducted. This section must describe:

- o When the files will be converted and/or created.
- o Organizational changes required during and after installation.
- o What reassignments of workloads are required during and after installation.
- o What contingency plans have been developed for installation failure.

3. Responsibilities

Responsibilities for the activities conducted during the installation phase.

EXAMPLE

INSTALLATION PLAN

PERSONNEL/PAYROLL PROJECT 402

DATE: 01/02/XX

FROM: R. Smith

TO: R. Neuf

1. SCOPE

The Personnel/Payroll System will be installed in its entirety. If all report programs are not ready, those portions not required for 3 or 6 months will be installed by the 3- or 6-month period.

Where applicable, installation of parts of the system will be companywide.

2. APPROACH

Final conversion of old system data to new will take place one month prior to production under the new system. From that point on, the new system file must be maintained on a current basis with all other payroll and personnel files. All new forms must be in use one month before production, or earlier if possible or if we are out of old forms. Exception time reporting must be installed companywide during June and be effective July 1, 19XX.

During installation, current employees must function as coders and terminal operators. After installation, the two operating units (payroll and personnel) will merge into one under one supervisor.

During installation added help and extra time will be required to maintain the old and new systems. Existing staff is sufficient if stenographic work is done by HO Steno and noncritical clerical work is postponed until after installation. After installation, the payroll reports for the second quarter must be prepared and, depending on the operation of the new system, 4 payroll processing clerks should be available for reassignment. The data processing workload will be decreased by eliminating personnel masterfile (card) and time card processing.

In the event of installation failure, the present system will be continued.

3. RESPONSIBILITY

The Manager of Employee Compensation is responsible for the installation of the exception time reporting system. The Payroll Supervisor is responsible for authorizing payroll production after parallel runs and for the operation of the video and typewriter terminals. He is also responsible for the coding of all input to the system. The project development team is responsible for all assistance and training needed during installation.

REPORT DISPLAY WORKSHEET

SYSTEM NAME ____________ REPORT TITLE ____________ USER NAME ____________

	CONTROL FIELDS (Major Thru Minor)				INFORMATION FIELDS						
New Page	Yes No	Yes No	Yes No	Yes No							
Take Total	Yes No	Yes No	Yes No	Yes No							
In Sequence	Yes No	Yes No	Yes No	Yes No							
Field Content											
Data Source											

Preparation Frequency		Report Has Value Because:	Prepared By Date
When Reset	Transaction Data Will Be ☐ Detail Listed ☐ Summarized		EDP Approval Date
Lines Printed	Calculation Description:	Report Will Be Used By:	User Approval Date

Figure 30
(Page 1 of 5)

Figure 30
(Page 2 of 5)

REPORT DISPLAY WORKSHEET

(1) SYSTEM NAME ______ (2) REPORT TITLE ______ (3) USER NAME ______

	CONTROL FIELDS (Major Thru Minor) (4)				INFORMATION FIELDS (5)						
(6) New Page	Yes No	Yes No	Yes No	Yes No							
(7) Take Total	Yes No	Yes No	Yes No	Yes No							
(8) In Sequence	Yes No	Yes No	Yes No	Yes No							
(9) Field Content											
(10) Data Source											

(11) Preparation Frequency		Report Has Value Because: (16)	Prepared By (18) Date
	Transaction Data Will Be (14) ☐ Detail Listed ☐ Summarized		
(12) When Reset			EDP Approval (19) Date
(13) Lines Printed	Calculation Description: (15)	Report Will Be Used By: (17)	
			User Approval (20) Date

INSTRUCTIONS FOR FORM: REPORT DISPLAY WORKSHEET

DEFINITION OF EACH ELEMENT:

KEY	ELEMENT/CONTENT
1.	System Name Name assigned.
2.	Report Title Title and/or number of report
3.	User Name User for whom this report is being prepared.
4.	Control Fields Identifies name of data that control report logic. Generally located at left portion of report printout.
5.	Information Fields Identifies name of data that will be acted upon by control fields.
6.	New Page Identifies whether control-field changes necessitate a new page.
7.	Take Total Identifies whether totals should be taken upon change of control-field data.
8.	In Sequence Identifies whether specific control-field data should be sorted.
9.	Field Content Identifies all data as to whether alpha or numeric.
10.	Data Source Identifies all files from which report data are obtained.

INSTRUCTIONS FOR FORM: REPORT DISPLAY WORKSHEET--Continued

DEFINITION OF EACH ELEMENT:

KEY	ELEMENT/CONTENT
11.	Preparation Frequency Anticipated frequency of preparation.
12.	When Reset Time period at which data should be deleted from presentation.
13.	Lines Printed Estimate of print volume to be generated.
14.	Transaction Data Will Be Identifies whether report data should be summarized or printed in detail.
15.	Calculation Description Describes any calculation logic, where appropriate.
16.	Report Has Value Because Identifies purpose and usefulness of report.
17.	Report Will Be Used By Identifies personnel or function that will use report.
18.	Prepared By Signature of analyst preparing the worksheet. Includes date of preparation.
19.	EDP Approval Signature of data processing approving authority. Includes date of approval.
20.	User Approval Signature of user approval authority. Includes date of approval.

EXAMPLE

Figure 30
(Page 5 of 5)

REPORT DISPLAY WORKSHEET

SYSTEM NAME	REPORT TITLE	USER NAME
Sales Analysis	Trade Class Regional Sales Trend	Marketing

	CONTROL FIELDS (Major Thru Minor)				INFORMATION FIELDS						
	Trade Class	Region	Product		Description	Sales This YTD	Sales This Mo.	Sales Last Mo.	Sales 2 Mos. Ago	Sales 3 Mos. Ago	Sales 4 Mos. Ago
					Trade Class, Region						
New Page	[Yes] No	Yes [No]	Yes No	Yes No							
Take Total	[Yes] No	Yes No	[Yes] No	Yes No							
In Sequence	[Yes] No	Yes No	Yes No	Yes No							
Field Content	1 pos.	3 pos.	1 pos.								
Data Source	Cust. Master	Invoice	Invoice		Table						

Preparation Frequency: Monthly		Report Has Value Because: Sales trend by region required by sales mgmt.	Prepared By: R. Jones — Date: 8/12/XX
When Reset:	Transaction Data Will Be: ☐ Detail Listed ☒ Summarized		EDP Approval: A. Able — Date: 8/14/XX
Lines Printed: 160	Calculation Description:	Report Will Be Used By: Mr. Brown, Mr. Lee; Product Managers	User Approval: G. Brown — Date: 8/24/XX

Figure 31
(Page 1 of 5)

PROJECT COST CONTROL

PROJECT NUMBER ______________________

PROJECT NAME ______________________

BUDGET DOLLARS			
TOTAL	ANALYST	PROGRAMMER	TEST TIME

DATE: ____________

DEPTS.: ____________

USER: ____________

WEEK ENDING	ANALYST/PROGRAMMER BUDGET NAME ____ RATE ____		BUDGET NAME ____ RATE ____		BUDGET NAME ____ RATE ____		BUDGET NAME ____ RATE ____		EQPT. OPER. COSTS			WEEKLY TOTAL	CUMULATIVE TOTAL
	Hours	$	Hours	$	Hours	$	Hours	$					

PROJECT COST CONTROL

PROJECT NUMBER ________ (2)

PROJECT NAME ________ (3)

BUDGET DOLLARS			
TOTAL (4)	ANALYST	PROGRAMMER	TEST TIME

DATE: ________ (1)

DEPTS.: ________ (5)

USER: ________ (6)

WEEK ENDING	ANALYST/PROGRAMMER												
	BUDGET (7)		BUDGET		BUDGET		BUDGET						
	NAME ____ (8) RATE ____		NAME ____ RATE ____		NAME ____ RATE ____		NAME ____ RATE ____		EQPT.	OPER.	COSTS	WEEKLY TOTAL	CUMULATIVE TOTAL
	Hours	$	Hours	$	Hours	$	Hours	$					
(9)	(10)								(11)			(12)	(13)

INSTRUCTIONS FOR FORM:

PROJECT COST CONTROL

DEFINITION OF EACH ELEMENT:

KEY	ELEMENT/CONTENT
1.	Date Date this sheet was prepared.
2.	Project Number Number assigned to the project.
3.	Project Name Name assigned to the project.
4.	Budget Dollars Total dollars associated with this project. Also includes provision for identification of anticipated costs by analyst, programmer, and machine testing categories.
5.	Departments Departments to be charged for services rendered.
6.	User Name(s) of key user personnel associated with the project.
7.	Budget The amount of time and/or dollars associated with individuals assigned to the project.

INSTRUCTIONS FOR FORM:

PROJECT COST CONTROL--continued

DEFINITION OF EACH ELEMENT:

KEY	**ELEMENT/CONTENT**
8.	Name/Rate Name of the analyst and/or programmers assigned to the project. Hourly rate assigned to the individual or job class is also identified for subsequent costing of actual progress.
9.	Week Ending Period of time that actual hours were incurred on the project.
10.	Hours, Dollars Actual hours incurred by each individual assigned to the project for the time period identified. Hours are multiplied by the rate to obtain actual costs incurred.
11.	Equipment and Operational Costs Any costs regarding equipment, data entry, computer run time, etc. are identified and recorded here.
12.	Weekly Total Total costs incurred for the week or time period.
13.	Cumulative Total Cumulative costs associated to date on the project.

Figure 31
(Page 5 of 5)

EXAMPLE

PROJECT COST CONTROL

PROJECT NUMBER 7069

PROJECT NAME Supplies Inventory

DATE: 1/5/XX

BUDGET DOLLARS			
TOTAL	ANALYST	PROGRAMMER	TEST TIME
$25,000	$10,000	$9,000	$4,800

DEPTS.: 204

USER: J. Scolozi

WEEK ENDING	ANALYST/PROGRAMMER												
	BUDGET $275 NAME E. Nagel RATE $40		BUDGET $10,000 NAME R. Jones RATE $36		BUDGET $9,000 NAME N. Girard RATE $29		BUDGET NAME RATE		EQPT.	OPER.	COSTS	WEEKLY TOTAL	CUMULATIVE TOTAL
	Hours	$	Hours	$	Hours	$	Hours	$	CRT				
1/14	1	40	3	108								148	148
1/21			35	1,260	4	116						1,376	1,524
1/28			28	1,008	7	203			100			1,311	2,835

III

TECHNICAL DOCUMENTATION

Technical documentation provides a comprehensive and detailed outline of a system's technical concepts, design, and operation. It is used primarily by technical personnel to maintain, modify, and enhance the system. The documentation consists of a number of standard components, some in narrative form and others in predefined formats. To remain useful and accurate, it is imperative that technical documentation be maintained in concert with system modifications and enhancements. Documentation updates are an integral part of systems maintenance activities.

The specific components of technical documentation include the following:

- System overview (Figure 32)
- System flowchart and flowchart narrative (Figure 33)
- File specifications (Figures 34, 35, and 36)
- General description of computer jobs/programs (Figure 37)
- Program function (Figures 38 and 39)
- Modification log (Figure 40)
- Program source listing (Figure 41)
- Job control listing (Figure 42)
- Information matrix (Figure 43)
- Tape and disk requirements sheet (Figure 44)
- Program test history record (Figure 45)
- Program test results (Figure 46)
- Decision table (Figure 47)

Each of these components is briefly described below. Required forms are illustrated and described in the forms section. The forms section includes a sample of each required form, detailed instructions for preparation, and an example of completed forms. Examples of narrative-format components are also given.

System overview. The system overview is a free-form, high-level description of the system's design objectives, concepts, and structure. It is intended to give the reader an overview of the system from the technical and application points of view. Objectives, scope, and design concepts (from the functional design specifications) should be addressed, as well as processing and operational considerations such as subsystems, frequency of operation, volume of data, and hardware/software requirements.

System flowchart and flowchart narrative. The system flowchart is a graphic representation of a system's processing steps. The charts are intended to present the logical flow of program steps within the system. Each subsystem of related programs should be presented on a separate flowchart.

File specifications. File specifications define the attributes, content, and format of all data files used in a system. Each file is defined on three file specification forms to identify contents, usage, and format. Every system file, including transaction files, master files, work files, and logging files, requires a separate file specification form.

General description of computer jobs/programs. This document describes all the jobs and programs in the system in general, nontechnical terms.

Program function. The program-function form includes a brief description of the program's purpose, and identifies the files on which the program operates and the program's major functions. It serves as the program specification; if necessary, each program is further defined on a program-function note form. Each major program function, including file-handling logic, edit criteria, and calculations, must be documented. All transaction and report formats relevant to a program should also be referenced in this document. Utility and sort programs do not require program-function forms, unless user exit coding is employed.

Modification log. A modification log should be maintained in the system documentation. The log should include a brief description of the modification, the date it was made, who made it, and who authorized it. All affected documentation elements must be updated to reflect the modifications.

Program source listing. Listings of all application programs are an integral part of the system documentation. Such listings should be bound separately from the system documentation (because of their size) and appear in the same sequence as the programs are presented in the system flowchart. There is no specific form for the program listing, since it is generated by the compiler. It must be an error-free program listing (with initialed warnings, if appropriate) which contains the compilation date, program name, program number,and programmer name.

Job control listing. Listings of all job control language necessary to execute system processing streams are also a part of system documentation. Such listings should be bound with program listings, in the same sequence as processing streams are presented on the system flowchart. The job control list will be the most recent list produced by the computer, in standard format. It should be replaced by a new list whenever the job control statements are changed.

Information matrix. This document is used to present the interrelationships between output records, input data, data elements, and files. The matrix can be used during either analysis or design activities and can also be used to specify relationships between files, record structures, and programs.

Tape and disk requirements sheet. This is used to specify the number and retention period of tapes, disks, and diskettes required in the system.

Program test history record. This is used to record the progress in development of new programs and subsequent testing as a result of revisions.

Program test results. Consists of actual results of the program being tested.

Decision table. This document provides a comprehensible format for logical decisions required by a system. Specific actions as a result of predefined conditions are noted in a format amenable to program modules.

INSTRUCTIONS FOR FORM:

SYSTEM OVERVIEW

DEFINITION OF EACH ELEMENT:

KEY	ELEMENT/CONTENT
1.	System Narrative Summary of various design concepts, objectives and structures that evolved through the conceptual and functional design stages.
2.	Major System Features Presents recaps of input transactions and volumes plus features of the system.
3.	Major Reports Presents recaps of key reports derived from the system, plus frequencies of issuance.

NOTE: The system overview provides an introduction to detail documentation that follows. Previously developed statements of Introduction, Objectives, Scope and Design Concepts may serve this purpose if design has not varied much from inception through development.

EXAMPLE

SYSTEM OVERVIEW

INVENTORY

System Narrative

(1) The purpose of the proposed Inventory Control System is the maintenance of accurate inventory balances for all raw materials and finished goods. Inventory information concerning availability must be on-line. The system is based on a Bill-of-Materials, which provides relational data for nearly 400 end products. Multiple inventory locations and the ability to identify customers on the basis of data on "from warehouse" shipments are features which the system must provide. The Inventory System should provide:

1. On-line inventory maintenance of quantity produced, quantity on order, quantity "in transit," and amount reserved.
2. Selective inventory status reports which highlight inventory shortages and exceptions.
3. On-line activity reporting and audit.
4. Inventory value classifications (ABC) and maintenance of economic order quantities (EOQs).

(2) Major System Features

1. Input Transactions:

Name/Input Mode	Volume
a. Receipts (on-line entry)	100/day
b. Shipments (on-line entry)	1,200/day
c. Returns	100/day
d. Production Completions	20/day
e. Cycle Counts	4,000/day
f. Adjustments (on-line entry)	20/day
g. Check-ins	50/day

2. Automated Features:

   a. The system must maintain inventory for multiple locations.

   b. The Bill-of-Materials must be able to accept "same-as-except" build transactions when variation in production standard (raw materials) to actual occurs.

EXAMPLE

Figure 32
(Page 3 of 3)

c. The system must be capable of identifying lot numbers and product type coding.

d. Monthly ABC analysis should be a capability of the system as well as EOQ computation.

e. Maintenance of the following data items:

- Quantity on Hand
- Quantity in Transit
- Quantity Committed
- Lead Time
- Safety Stock
- Reorder Point
- Sales History
- Volumes by Cases

f. The Inventory System should automatically interface with the Cost and Sales Analysis systems in a data base environment.

g. The system will require the addition of two CRT terminals.

(3) Major Reports

Major Reports	Frequency
1. Summarized Bill-of-Materials • Indented • Where-used list	Weekly
2. Inventory Report • On-line Details by Product • By Warehouse • Raw Materials • Finished Goods	Daily
3. Inventory Management Report • Month's Sales; Cases, Dollars • ABC Ranking	Monthly
4. Basic Edit/Update Reports	Daily
5. File Inquiry Capability through Systems Software	Interactive

Figure 33

INSTRUCTIONS FOR FORM: SYSTEM FLOWCHART AND FLOWCHART NARRATIVE

DEFINITION OF EACH ELEMENT:

KEY	ELEMENT/CONTENT

NOTE: Technical documentation under this heading represents updated information in the format described under System Flowchart and System Flowchart Narrative.

Please refer to Figures 7 and 8.

Figure 34
(Page 1 of 5)

FILE SPECIFICATION CONTENTS	
PREPARED BY:	DATE:
FILE ID:	
FILE NAME:	Page of

DESCRIPTION

SPECIFICATION

ORGANIZATION:

RECORD LENGTH:

BLOCKING FACTOR:

MEDIUM:

VOLUME:

RETENTION:

KEY:

Figure 34
(Page 2 of 5)

FILE SPECIFICATION CONTENTS	
PREPARED BY: (1)	DATE: (2)
FILE ID: (3)	
FILE NAME: (4)	Page of

DESCRIPTION

(5)

SPECIFICATION

ORGANIZATION: (6) thru (12)

RECORD LENGTH:

BLOCKING FACTOR:

MEDIUM:

VOLUME:

RETENTION:

KEY:

INSTRUCTIONS FOR FORM: FILE SPECIFICATION--CONTENTS

DEFINITION OF EACH ELEMENT:

KEY	ELEMENT/CONTENT
1.	Prepared By Person who prepared the form.
2.	Date Date of preparation.
3.	File ID File identification code as it appears on job control language and program listings.
4.	File Name Brief descriptive name for this file.
5.	Description Brief narrative description of the file's purpose, structure, and content.
6.	Organization Identifies the access method (e.g., sequential, ISAM, etc.) for this file.
7.	Record Length Identifies the record length in characters for logical file records. If a variable-length file, express as a range.
8.	Blocking Factor The number of logical records contained in a physical data block.
9.	Medium The medium that this file resides on (e.g., card, disk, etc.).

INSTRUCTIONS FOR FORM: FILE SPECIFICATION--CONTENTS--Continued

DEFINITION OF EACH ELEMENT:

KEY	ELEMENT/CONTENT
10.	Volume An approximate average volume of logical records in this file. If the volume is highly time-dependent, volume should be expressed as a range (low-high).
11.	Retention The period of time, or number of processing cycles, that this file should be retained after creation.
12.	Key Specifies the location of the key to the file in the logical record, the field names contained in the key, and their location in the logical record.

EXAMPLE

FILE SPECIFICATION CONTENTS

PREPARED BY: J. Wells | **DATE:** 3/12/XX

FILE ID: AROIM

FILE NAME: On-line Accounts Receivable Open Items Master | **Page** 1 **of** 3

DESCRIPTION

Each record contains up to seven items for a customer. If an occupant has more than seven invoices during a month, there will be more than one record.

SPECIFICATION

ORGANIZATION:	ISAM
RECORD LENGTH:	425 BYTES
BLOCKING FACTOR:	2 RECORDS PER BLOCK
MEDIUM:	DISK
VOLUME:	30,000
RETENTION:	PERMANENT (RELOAD DAILY)
KEY:	2-22

COMPANY NUMBER:	2-4
CUSTOMER ID.:	5-11
TYPE ID.:	12-18
GEOGRAPHIC NUMBER:	19-19
RECORD CODE:	20-20
SEQUENCE #:	21-22

Figure 35
(Page 1 of 4)

FILE SPECIFICATION USAGE

PREPARED BY:	DATE:
FILE ID:	PAGE ___ OF ___

PROGRAMS WHERE USED

NAME	HOW USED	COMMENTS

SIGNIFICANT FIELDS

Figure 35
(Page 2 of 4)

FILE SPECIFICATION USAGE	
PREPARED BY: (1)	DATE: (2)
FILE ID: (3)	PAGE __ OF __

PROGRAMS WHERE USED

NAME (4)	HOW USED (5)	COMMENTS (6)

SIGNIFICANT FIELDS (7)

INSTRUCTIONS FOR FORM: FILE SPECIFICATION USAGE

DEFINITION OF EACH ELEMENT:

KEY	ELEMENT/CONTENT
1.	Prepared By Person who prepared the form.
2.	Date Date of preparation.
3.	File ID File identification code as it appears in job control language and program listings.
4.	Name Listing of names of programs using this file.
5.	How Used Identifies for each program how this file is used (input, output, and so on).
6.	Comments A one-line description of the file's use in each program.
7.	Significant Fields A brief narrative description of fields in the logical record that require more definition than their name.

EXAMPLE

FILE SPECIFICATION USAGE

PREPARED BY: J. Wells

DATE: 3/12/XX

FILE ID: AROIM

PAGE 2 **OF** 4

PROGRAMS WHERE USED

NAME	HOW USED	COMMENTS
AR720	Update	New Recurring Charges
AR740	Input	Back-up
AR745	Output	Reload
AR11	Update	Cash Payments
AR12	Update	Miscellaneous Charges

SIGNIFICANT FIELDS

Record, Amount, and Potential
Up to seven occurrences of these fields on any record.
Amount--The dollar amount of the transaction.
Potential--If this is a charge of services, this field contains the potential gain.
Transaction Type--Three valid transactions:

O--Charges to receivables
P--Payments for receivables
S--Security transactions

INSTRUCTIONS FOR FORM: FILE SPECIFICATION RECORD FORMAT

DEFINITION OF EACH ELEMENT:

KEY **ELEMENT/CONTENT**

NOTE: Technical documentation under this heading should represent updated information in the format described under Functional Design Specification.

Please refer to Figures 13 and 14.

GENERAL DESCRIPTION OF COMPUTER JOBS/PROGRAMS

DATE PREPARED: ____________________

SYSTEM NAME: ____________________

PREPARED BY: ____________________

JOB NAME	PROGRAM NAME	ESTIMATED RUNNING TIME & FREQUENCY	GENERAL DESCRIPTION

GENERAL DESCRIPTION OF COMPUTER JOBS/PROGRAMS

DATE PREPARED: ______ (1)

SYSTEM NAME: ______ (2)

PREPARED BY: ______ (3)

JOB NAME	PROGRAM NAME	ESTIMATED RUNNING TIME & FREQUENCY	GENERAL DESCRIPTION
(4)	(5)	(6)	(7)

INSTRUCTIONS FOR FORM: GENERAL DESCRIPTION OF COMPUTER JOBS/PROGRAMS

DEFINITION OF EACH ELEMENT:

KEY	ELEMENT/CONTENT
1.	Date Prepared Date this list is prepared.
2.	System Name Name assigned.
3.	Prepared By Person who prepared this list.
4.	Job Name Linkage of programs by job stream.
5.	Program Name Assigned.
6.	Estimated Running Time and Frequency Estimated length of program's running time in minutes, and how often it is run (for example, 12 minutes/daily).
7.	General Description Describe in general terms what the program will do. Use language that can be understood by people who are not computer-oriented.

EXAMPLE

GENERAL DESCRIPTION OF COMPUTER JOBS/PROGRAMS

DATE PREPARED: 10/15/XX

SYSTEM NAME: Accounts Payable

PREPARED BY: E. Schwartz

JOB NAME	PROGRAM NAME	ESTIMATED RUNNING TIME & FREQUENCY	GENERAL DESCRIPTION
XFAPWIOW	APW01	25 min/weekly	Validation Run. Reads sorted Accounts Payable details, compares them to the Vendor Master File for validity. Prints an error listing and selects errors for manual correction, and writes a valid Accounts Payable Transaction File for further processing.
	APW02	10 min/weekly	Tape Sort. Sorts the Accounts Payable Transaction file from APW01 into Account order by Vendor for input into XFAPW20.
XFAPW20W	APW05	60 min/weekly	Voucher Register. Processes sorted Accounts Payable Transactions and the Vendor File to produce an Accounts Payable Distribution Tape, a Voucher Register, a Bank Reconciliation File and a Check Processing File.

Figure 38
(Page 1 of 5)

PROGRAM FUNCTION

CLIENT/DEPARTMENT			PAGE OF
SYSTEM			REVISION DATE
PROGRAM NAME	NO.	PREPARED BY	DATE

DESCRIPTION:

INPUT FILES

	FILE NAME	NO.	MEDIA
1.			
2.			
3.			
4.			
5.			
6.			

PROGRAM FUNCTIONS

NO.	FUNCTION DESCRIPTION	PROGRAM FUNCTION NOTE

*Assign a program function note number to refer to associated program function note sheet(s).

OUTPUT FILES

	FILE NAME	NO.	MEDIA
1.			
2.			
3.			
4.			
5.			
6.			

Figure 38
(Page 2 of 5)

EXAMPLE

PROGRAM FUNCTION

CLIENT/DEPARTMENT (1)			PAGE (8) OF
SYSTEM (2)			REVISION DATE (7)
PROGRAM NAME (3)	NO. (4)	PREPARED BY (5)	DATE (6)

DESCRIPTION:
(9)

INPUT FILES

	FILE NAME	NO.	MEDIA
1.	(10)		
2.			
3.			
4.			
5.			
6.			

PROGRAM FUNCTIONS

NO.	FUNCTION DESCRIPTION	PROGRAM FUNCTION NOTE
	(11)	

•Assign a program function note number to refer to associated program function note sheet(s).

OUTPUT FILES

	FILE NAME	NO.	MEDIA
1.	(12)		
2.			
3.			
4.			
5.			
6.			

INSTRUCTIONS FOR FORM: PROGRAM FUNCTION

DEFINITION OF EACH ELEMENT:

KEY **ELEMENT/CONTENT**

1. Client/Department

   Name of the user department or corporate entity to which this program is applicable.

2. System

   Name of the system in which this program is included.

3. Program Name

   Name by which this program is identified in the system.

4. No.

   Program number, if different from program name.

5. Prepared By

   Name of the person who prepared this program function form.

6. Date

   Date that this form was prepared.

7. Revision Date

   If this form was revised, the date of the latest revision.

8. Page

   Page sequence and total number. Any additional documents, such as the program function notes, required to support the program function must be included in total page count.

9. Description

   Brief description of the program, including its intended function, language, and frequency of operation.

10. Input Files

    Names of all files used as input to this program. Include identification numbers (for reference use in program function notes) and file's resident media.

INSTRUCTIONS FOR FORM: PROGRAM FUNCTION--Continued

DEFINITION OF EACH ELEMENT:

KEY	ELEMENT/CONTENT
11.	Program Functions One-line descriptions of major program functions, with identifying reference numbers, and a reference to a more detailed function description, if required, on the program function notes form.
12.	Output Files Names of all files output from this program. Include identification numbers (for reference use in program function notes) and the file's resident media.

Figure 38
(Page 5 of 5)

EXAMPLE

PROGRAM FUNCTION

CLIENT/DEPARTMENT XYZ Company			PAGE 1 OF 3
SYSTEM Accounts Receivable			REVISION DATE
PROGRAM NAME Customer File Charges	NO. AR0415	PREPARED BY J. Smith	DATE 11/3/XX

DESCRIPTION:
Subsystem(s): Closing update master files
Prints recurring charges; creates tape of recurring charges

INPUT FILES

	FILE NAME	NO.	MEDIA
1.	SELECTF--Properties to be printed		Tape
2.	AIUMSTF--On-line unit customer master		Disk
3.	TMSF03 --Product Master		Disk
4.			
5.			
6.			

PROGRAM FUNCTIONS

NO.	FUNCTION DESCRIPTION	PROGRAM FUNCTION NOTE
	If SELECTF cards entered (U1 ON) will only process those products.	
	If U2 ON--'cut-off balance run'	
	U2 OFF--create output tape	

**Assign a program function note number to refer to associated program function note sheet(s).*

OUTPUT FILES

	FILE NAME	NO.	MEDIA
1.	ARCHRGE--Recurring charges file		Tape
2.	PRINT--"Recurring charges master control"		PTR
3.			
4.			
5.			
6.			

Figure 39
(Page 1 of 4)

PROGRAM FUNCTION NOTES

CLIENT/DEPARTMENT	DATE PREPARED	PAGE OF
SYSTEM NAME	PREPARED BY	
PROGRAM NAME & NO.	REVISED BY	DATE

PROGRAM FUNCTION NUMBER	DESCRIPTION

Figure 39
(Page 2 of 4)

PROGRAM FUNCTION NOTES

CLIENT/DEPARTMENT (1)	DATE PREPARED (4)	PAGE (9) OF
SYSTEM NAME (2)	PREPARED BY (5)	
PROGRAM NAME & NO. (3)	REVISED BY (6)	DATE (7)

PROGRAM FUNCTION NUMBER	DESCRIPTION
	(8)

INSTRUCTIONS FOR FORM:

PROGRAM FUNCTION NOTES

DEFINITION OF EACH ELEMENT:

KEY	ELEMENT/CONTENT
1.	Client/Department Name of the user department or corporate entity to which this program is applicable.
2.	System Name Name of the system in which this program is included.
3.	Program Name and No. Name by which this program is identified in the system, and program number if different from program name.
4.	Date Prepared Date that this program function notes form was prepared.
5.	Prepared By Name of the person who revised this form.
6.	Revised By Name of the person who prepared this form.
7.	Date Date of the last revision to this form.
8.	Description Program function descriptions, with program function numbers cross-referencing the descriptions to the program function form.
9.	Page Page sequence and total number.

Figure 39
(Page 4 of 4)

EXAMPLE

PROGRAM FUNCTION NOTES

CLIENT/DEPARTMENT	DATE PREPARED	PAGE
XYZ Company	11/3/XX	2 OF 3

SYSTEM NAME	PREPARED BY
Accounts Receivable	J. Smith

PROGRAM NAME & NO.	REVISED BY	DATE
AR0415		

PROGRAM FUNCTION NUMBER	DESCRIPTION
	ERRORS
	Start must occur prior to stop date
L1	Customer in AIUMSTF
L2	Unit in AIUMSTF
L3	Product in AIUMSTF and SELECTF
L4	Company in AIUMSTF and SELECTF
M1	Company, and product in AIUMSTF and SELECTF

Figure 40
(Page 1 of 4)

MODIFICATION LOG

SYSTEM NAME: ______________________________ Page___ of _____

IMPLEMENTATION DATE	IMPLEMENTATION BY	REQUESTED BY	PROGRAM (if appl.)	DESCRIPTION

MODIFICATION LOG

(1) (2)

SYSTEM NAME: ______________________________ Page ___ of _____

IMPLEMENTATION DATE	IMPLEMENTATION BY	REQUESTED BY	PROGRAM (if appl.)	DESCRIPTION
(3)	(4)	(5)	(6)	(7)

INSTRUCTIONS FOR FORM: MODIFICATION LOG

DEFINITION OF EACH ELEMENT:

KEY	ELEMENT/CONTENT
1.	System Name Identification of the system that this log applies to.
2.	Page Number Sequential reference of modification log pages.
3.	Implementation Date The date that this modification was put into effect.
4.	Implementation By Identifies the person who made this modification.
5.	Requested By Identifies the person authorizing this modification.
6.	Program The program(s) affected by this modification, if applicable.
7.	Description Brief narrative description of the modification.

EXAMPLE

Figure 40
(Page 4 of 4)

MODIFICATION LOG

SYSTEM NAME: Accounts Receivable Page 1 of ____

IMPLEMENTATION DATE	IMPLEMENTATION BY	REQUESTED BY	PROGRAM (if appl.)	DESCRIPTION
3/2/XX	R. Smith	J. Baum	AR0415	Change Age Logic and Column Headings from 10-30-45 Days to 30-60-90.

EXAMPLE

Figure 41

PROGRAM SOURCE LISTING

```
DOS PL/I COMPILER  360N-PL-464 CL3-4              SUISYS              06/08/               PAGE 002

SUTA12: PROCEDURE( A, IPROC, VK );

  1        SUTA12: PROCEDURE( A, IPROC, VK );                                         UT201025
           /*                                                                        */UT201050
           /* GENERALYZED UPCATE  CONTROL                                            */UT201075
           /*                                                                        */UT201100
           /* PARAMETER AREAS                                                        */UT201125
           /*                                                                        */UT201150
  2              DCL A( 4000 )  FIXED BINARY;                                         UT201175
           /*                                                                        */UT201200
  3              DCL IPROC      CHAR( 1 );                                            UT201225
           /*                                                                        */UT201250
  4              DCL VK( 20 )   CHAR( 15 );                                           UT201275
           /*                                                                        */UT201300
           /* WORK AREAS                                                             */UT201325
           /*                                                                        */UT201350
  5              DCL CSV( 1134 ) STATIC CHAR( 1 );                                    UT201375
           /*                                                                        */UT201400
  6              DCL( LINE,                                                           UT201425
                      IPG,                                                            UT201430
                      ILAST,                                                          UT201450
                      IMATCH,                                                         UT201475
                      ICNT ) STATIC FIXED BINARY;                                     UT201500
           /*                                                                        */UT210025
           /* MAIN                                                                   */UT210050
           /*                                                                        */UT210075
  7              IPG = 0;                                                             UT210080
  8              LINE = 99;                        /* INITIALYZE                     */UT210100
  9              ILAST = 0;                        /* LAST                           */UT210125
 10              IMATCH = 0;                       /* ROUTINE #                      */UT210150
 11              ICNT = 0;                         /* START OF DATA                  */UT210155
 12              DO I = 1 TO 4000;                                                    UT210160
 13                A( I ) = 0;                                                        UT210165
 14              END;                                                                 UT210170
 15        RDCDS:                                                                     UT210175
                 CALL SUTAA2( IPROC, VK, CSV, LINE, ILAST, IMATCH, ICNT, IPG ); UT210200
 16              IF ILAST ¬= 0 THEN                /* CHECK END                      */UT210205
                   RETURN;                                                            UT210210
 17              IF IMATCH > 11 THEN                                                  UT210225
                   GC TO RDCDS;                                                       UT210250
 18              IF IMATCH > 5 THEN                /* CHECK WHICH CONTROL            */UT210275
                   GO TO GT5;                      /* P-12-050                       */UT210300
 19              IF IMATCH > 3 THEN                                                   UT210325
                   GC TO GT3;                      /* P-11-300                       */UT210350
 20              IF IMATCH > 1 THEN                                                   UT210375
                   GC TO GT1;                      /* P-11-050                       */UT210400
 21              CALL CVERLAY( 'SUT120' );         /* MASTER                         */UT210425
 22              CALL SUTA20( A, IPROC, CSV, LINE, ICNT, IPG );                       UT210450
 23              GO TO RDCDS;                      /* P-10-175                       */UT211455
 24        GT1:                                                                       UT211050
                 IF IMATCH = 3 THEN                                                   UT211075
                   GC TO EQ3;                      /* P-11-200                       */UT211100
 25              CALL OVERLAY( 'SUT121' );         /* TRANSACTION                    */UT211125
 26              CALL SUTA21( A, IPROC, CSV, LINE, ICNT, IPG );                       UT211150
 27              GO TO RDCDS;                      /* P-10-175                       */UT211175
 28        EQ3:                                                                       UT211200
                 CALL OVERLAY( 'SUT122' );         /* CONSTANTS                      */UT211225
```

Figure 42

EXAMPLE

JOB CONTROL LISTING

```
//BECKER   JOB (95022),'CASE 9980-887',MSGLEVEL=(1,1),MSGCLASS=5,
// CLASS=Z,TIME=3
LOG IEF403I BECKER   STARTED TIME=00.48.18
LOG BECKER   PRINT    00.48.17 00.49.48     90    34.76 C0000
LOG IEF404I BECKER   ENDED   TIME=00.49.48
***
//PRINT   EXEC PGM=IEBPTPCH,REGION=60K
***
***     PRINTS IPA EXPANDED LIST ON 3800 PRINTER
***
//SYSIN    DD *
//SYSPRINT DD SYSOUT=5
//SYSUT1   DD DSNAME=IPA.SOURCE.IMAGES,
//            DISP=SHR,
//            UNIT=3350,
//            VOLUME=(,RETAIN,SER=T00143)
//SYSUT2   DD SYSOUT=5,DCB=LRECL=133,COPIES=001
//
IEF236I ALLOC. FOR BECKER   PRINT
IEF237I 143    ALLOCATED TO SYSUT1
IEF142I - STEP WAS EXECUTED - COND CODE 0000
IEF285I   IPA.SOURCE.IMAGES                    KEPT
IEF285I   VOL SER NOS= T00143.
IEF373I STEP /PRINT   / START 78168.0048
IEF374I STEP /PRINT   / STOP  78168.0049 CPU   OMIN 34.76SEC STOR VIRT  36K
IEF298I  BECKER   SYSOUT=5.
IEF375I  JOB /BECKER  / START 78168.0048
IEF376I  JOB /BECKER  / STOP  78168.0049 CPU   OMIN 34.76SEC
```

Figure 43
(Page 1 of 4)

INFORMATION MATRIX

DATE PREPARED: __________

SYSTEM NAME: __________

SYSTEM NO.: __________ PREPARED BY: __________

DATA ELEMENTS	OUTPUT REPORTS						DATA SOURCE CODES
							INPUTS (I)
							FILES (F)
							CALCULATIONS

INFORMATION MATRIX

DATE PREPARED: ① ____________________

SYSTEM NAME: ② ____________________

SYSTEM NO.: ③ ____________________ PREPARED BY: ④ ____________________

⑥ DATA ELEMENTS	OUTPUT REPORTS ⑤						DATA SOURCE CODES
							INPUTS (I) ⑧
			⑦				FILES (F)
							CALCULATIONS

INSTRUCTIONS FOR FORM: INFORMATION MATRIX

DEFINITION OF EACH ELEMENT:

KEY	ELEMENT/CONTENT
1.	Date Prepared Date the Matrix was prepared.
2.	System Name Name assigned to the system.
3.	System Number Number assigned to the system.
4.	Prepared By Person who prepared the Matrix.
5.	Horizontal Axis Category of data being reported-for example, a list of reports.
6.	Vertical Axis Data Elements being reported.
7.	Axis Coordinates The relationship between data on horizontal axis and data on vertical axis.
8.	Data Source Codes Provides a legend or key for interpreting the axis coordinates.

EXAMPLE

Figure 43
(Page 4 of 4)

INFORMATION MATRIX

DATE PREPARED: 3/16/XX

SYSTEM NAME: Payroll Reporting

SYSTEM NO.: 553 PREPARED BY: P. Schneid

DATA ELEMENTS	OUTPUT REPORTS: Audit Report	Error Listing	Employee Master (on Req.)	Payroll Regis.	Payroll Stub	
Employee Name		11,12 C1	F1	F3	11,12 13,14 15	
Employee Address		11	F1			
Employee Soc. Ins. #		11	F1			
Employee Dept. No.		11,12	F1		12,13	
Employee Occupation		12,13	F1		12,13	
Employee Hrly. Rate		13	F1		F1	
Federal Tax Exempt.		11	F1			
Prov. Tax Exemption		11	F1			
Pay Period Fed. Tax	F4		F1/ C2	F3	C2	
Pay Period State Tax	F4		F1/ C3	F3	C3	
Pay Period Gross	F4		F1/ C4	F3	C4	
Pay Period Net	F4		F1/ C5	F3	C5	
Pay Period U.I.C.	F4		F1/ C6	F3	C6	
Pay Period Fed. Pens.	F4		F1/ C7	F3	C7	
Pay Period State Pens.	F4		F1/ C8	F3	C8	
Pay Period Co. Pens.	F4		F1/ C9	F3	C9	
Y.T.D. Fed. Tax	F4		F1/ C10	F3		
Y.T.D. State Tax	F4		F1/ C11	F3		
Y.T.D. Gross	F4		F1/ C12	F3		
Y.T.D. Net	F4		F1/ C13	F3		

DATA SOURCE CODES

INPUTS (I)

11--Employee Status Form
12--Daily Time Sheet
13--Change Employee Status Form
14--Adjustment
15--Deduction

FILES (F)

F1--Employee Master File
F2--Daily Payroll Transaction File
F3--M.T.D. Register File
F4--Audit Report

CALCULATIONS

C1 --Edit of Master File Data
C2 --Calc. P.P. Fed. Tax
C3 --Calc. P.P. State Tax
C4 --Calc. P.P. Gross Pay
C5 --Calc. P.P. Net Pay
C6 --Calc. P.P. U.I.C.
C7 --Calc. P.P. Fed. Pens.
C8 --Calc. P.P. State Pens.
C9 --Calc. P.P. Co. Pens.
C10--Calc. Y.T.D. Fed. Tax
C11--Calc. Y.T.D. State Tax
C12--Calc. Y.T.D. Gross
C13--Calc. Y.T.D. Net
C14--Calc. Y.T.D. U.I.C.
C15--Calc. Y.T.D. Fed. Pens.
C16--Calc. Y.T.D. State Pen.
C17--Calc. Y.T.D. Co. Pens.

TAPE AND DISK REQUIREMENTS SHEET

DATE PREPARED: ____________________

SYSTEM NAME: ____________________

SYSTEM NO.: ____________________ PREPARED BY: ____________________

FILE NAME	NUMBER	TYPE	SIZE	CYCLE	RETENTION	QTY.

TYPE = D-Disk, DK-Diskette, T-Tape

TAPE AND DISK REQUIREMENTS SHEET

(1)
DATE PREPARED: ______________________

(2)
SYSTEM NAME: ____

(3) (4)
SYSTEM NO.: ______________________ PREPARED BY: ______________________

FILE NAME	NUMBER	TYPE	SIZE	CYCLE	RETENTION	QTY.
(5)	(6)	(7)	(8)	(9)	(10)	(11)

TYPE = D-Disk, DJ-Diskette, T-Tape

INSTRUCTIONS FOR FORM: TAPE AND DISK REQUIREMENTS SHEET

DEFINITION OF EACH ELEMENT:

KEY	ELEMENT/CONTENT
1.	Date Prepared Identifies the date when the sheet was prepared.
2.	System Name Name assigned to the system.
3.	System Number Number assigned to the system.
4.	Prepared By Identifies the person who prepared the tape and disk requirements sheet.
5.	File Name Identifies the name of the file that is on the tape or disk.
6.	Number Identifies the number assigned to the tapes and disks as part of the header label.
7.	Type Identifies whether the file is on disk (D), diskette (DK), or tape (T).
8.	Size Describes the size of the file in number of reels or packs.
9.	Cycle Identifies the processing cycle of the file.

INSTRUCTIONS FOR FORM: TAPE AND DISK REQUIREMENTS SHEET--
Continued

DEFINITION OF EACH ELEMENT:

KEY	ELEMENT/CONTENT
10.	Retention Identifies the method and duration of retention.
11.	Quantity Identifies the total number of tapes or disks required to operate the system. This number is based on retention requirements.

EXAMPLE

Figure 44
(Page 5 of 5)

TAPE AND DISK REQUIREMENTS SHEET

DATE PREPARED: 1/5/XX

SYSTEM NAME: Accounts Payable

SYSTEM NO.: 104 PREPARED BY: A. Goldberg

FILE NAME	NUMBER	TYPE	SIZE	CYCLE	RETENTION	QTY.
A/P Distribution		T	3 Reels	Weekly	2 weeks	6
Vendor Master File		D	1 Pack	Weekly	Grandfather--Father --Son	3

TYPE = D-Disk, DK-Diskette, T-Tape

Figure 45
(Page 1 of 4)

PROGRAM TEST HISTORY RECORD

DATE PREPARED: ____________________

SYSTEM NAME: ____

PROGRAM NUMBER	PROGRAM NAME	PROGRAMMER

DATE	PROG'R INITIAL	ACTION		REASON FOR ACTION	TEST RESULTS	TEST TIME
		COMPILE	TEST			

PROGRAM TEST HISTORY RECORD

(1)

DATE PREPARED: ____________

(2)

SYSTEM NAME: ____________

PROGRAM NUMBER (3)	PROGRAM NAME (4)	PROGRAMMER (5)

DATE	PROG'R INITIAL	ACTION		REASON FOR ACTION	TEST RESULTS	TEST TIME
		COMPILE	TEST			
(6)	(7)	(8)		(9)	(10)	(11)

INSTRUCTIONS FOR FORM: PROGRAM TEST HISTORY RECORD

DEFINITION OF EACH ELEMENT:

KEY	ELEMENT/CONTENT
1.	Date Prepared Identifies the date when the sheet was originally prepared.
2.	System Name Name assigned to the system.
3.	Program Number Number assigned to the program.
4.	Program Name Identifies the name of the program.
5.	Programmer Person who developed the original program.
6.	Date The date that testing or compiling of the program was performed.
7.	Programmer Initial Initials of the programmer performing testing.
8.	Action--Compile and Test A check mark to indicate the type of activity performed.
9.	Reason for Action Identifies briefly the objective for testing.
10.	Test Results Identifies briefly the results of testing relative to the objective.
11.	Test Time Indicates the amount of time required for the test.

EXAMPLE

PROGRAM TEST HISTORY RECORD

DATE PREPARED: June 28, 19XX

SYSTEM NAME: Billing Analysis

PROGRAM NUMBER	PROGRAM NAME	PROGRAMMER
B001ABA	Copy Billing Analysis Files	G. Gordon

DATE	PROG'R INITIAL	ACTION		REASON FOR ACTION	TEST RESULTS	TEST TIME
		COMPILE	TEST			
2/19/XX	JAB	✓	✓	Revise Territory Code Conversion	Truncate of left position of Territory Code	5 Min.
2/20/XX	JAB	✓	✓	Revise Territory Code Conversion	Successful	5 Min.

INSTRUCTIONS FOR FORM: PROGRAM TEST RESULTS

DEFINITION OF EACH ELEMENT:

KEY **ELEMENT/CONTENT**

These results take the form of the output being tested, so no sample form is supplied. However, there must be a sample of the output results. If the results are tape or disk files, a tape or disk printout (not a dump) of the file (with every field in readable form) is required. The printout will contain the program name and number, output-file name and number, and programmer as well as the data.

Figure 47
(Page 1 of 4)

DECISION TABLE

SYSTEM NAME ______________________ PROGRAM NUMBER, NAME ______________

LOGIC AREA ____________________ PREPARED BY ____________ DATE PREPARED ________

CONDITION		1	2	3	4	5	6	7	8	9
A										
B										
C										
D										
E										
F										
G										
ACTION										
H										
I										
J										
K										
L										
M										
N										
O										
P										
Q										
R										

Figure 47
(Page 2 of 4)

DECISION TABLE

SYSTEM NAME ___(1)___ PROGRAM NUMBER, NAME ___(2)___

LOGIC AREA ___(3)___ PREPARED BY ___(4)___ DATE PREPARED ___(5)___

(6)

	CONDITION	1	2	3	4	5	6	7	8	9
A										
B										
C										
D										
E										
F										
G										
	ACTION									
H										
I										
J										
K										
L										
M										
N										
O										
P										
Q										
R										

(7)

INSTRUCTIONS FOR FORM:

DECISION TABLE

DEFINITION OF EACH ELEMENT:

KEY	ELEMENT/CONTENT
1.	System Name Name assigned to the system.
2.	Program Number, Name Identification of programs in which decision table logic is used.
3.	Logic Area Identification of process encompassed by the table.
4.	Prepared By Analyst who prepared the table.
5.	Date Prepared Date the table was prepared.
6.	Condition The types of conditions that may occur are identified. Grid at right indicates whether each of the conditions occurs (Y=yes, N=no) so that combinations of conditions may be acted upon accordingly.
7.	Action All actions that may be required to satisfy a combination of conditions are identified. In accordance with the various conditions identified above, specific program actions are identified.

DECISION TABLE

SYSTEM NAME Order Processing **PROGRAM NUMBER, NAME** ORD 035

LOGIC AREA Order Entry **PREPARED BY** A. Poschmann **DATE PREPARED** 3/24/XX

	CONDITION	1	2	3	4	5	6	7	8	9
A	Is Customer Number valid?	N	Y	Y	Y	Y	Y	Y	Y	
B	Is Salesperson code valid?	–	N	Y	Y	Y	Y	Y	Y	
C	Is Product Number valid?	–	–	N	Y	Y	Y	Y	Y	
D	Are all products in stock?	–	–	–	N	N	Y	Y	N	
E	Is partial order code equal to 1?	–	–	–	Y	N	Y	Y	Y	
F	Is credit OK?	–	–	–	Y	Y	Y	N	N	
G										
	ACTION									
H	Reject item. Reask question	X	X	X						
I	Flag for Credit Mgr. review before shipment							X	X	
J	Ship quantity available				X				X	
K	Backorder balance of order				X				X	
L	Do not ship incomplete orders					X				
M	Ship quantity ordered						X	X		
N										
O										
P										
Q										
R										

IV

OPERATIONAL DOCUMENTATION

Operational documentation provides information and instructions to computer operational personnel regarding the execution of job streams in a system. The documentation consists of a number of standard components, most in standardized formats. Specific components include:

- System overview (Figure 48)
- System flowchart and flowchart narrative (Figure 48)
- Job instructions, Type 1 and Type 2 (Figures 49 and 50)
- Job control listing (Figure 51)
- Console message listing (Figure 52)
- Input/output schedule (Figure 53)
- Clerical desk instructions (Figure 54)
- Data entry instructions (Figure 55)
- Remote terminal instructions (Figure 56)
- Remote job instructions (Figure 57)
- Program release (Figure 58)
- Request for D.P. operations support (Figure 59)
- Input/output control procedure (Figure 60)
- Log of control procedures performed (Figure 61)
- Tape library file history (Figure 62)
- Tapes to be scratched (Figure 63)
- EDP operations schedule (Figure 64)
- Computer operations problem report (Figure 65)
- Operations daily report (Figure 66)

Each of these components is briefly described below. Required forms are illustrated and described in the forms section. The forms section includes a sample of each required form, detailed instructions for preparation, and an example of completed forms. Narrative-format components are also illustrated.

<u>System overview</u>. The system overview is a free-form, high-level description of the system's design objectives, concepts, and structure. It is intended to give the reader an overview of the system from the technical and application points of view. The objectives, scope, and design concepts of the system should be addressed, as well as processing and operational considerations such as subsystems, frequency of operation, volume of data, and hardware/software requirements.

System flowchart and flowchart narrative. The system flowchart is a graphic representation of a system's processing steps. The system flow begins with relevant source documents and data-entry steps. Each processing, data sequencing, and data base back-up program is represented, and all files, reports, and on-line displays are shown as appropriate.

Job instructions, Type 1 and Type 2. Job instruction sheets should concisely describe the card files, tape files, disk files, and printer setup used by a job stream or program. Operator responses and restart/recovery procedures are documented with supplemental narrative, as required, for complete operator instructions. Samples of any reports to be produced requiring alignment or operator verification should be included. Several examples of job instruction sheets are included in the forms section.

Job control listing. Listings of job control language necessary to execute processing streams are an integral part of operations documentation in mainframe environments. Such listings should be bound in front of job instruction sheets for each application system.

Console message listing. Listings of console messages inform the computer operator what situations may occur and what action to take in each of those cases.

Input/output schedule. The schedule identifies the input and output time requirements for all jobs, programs, data handling, and communications activities for an application system.

Clerical desk instructions. The instructions present the specific steps required to perform a clerical activity. Describe what the activity is, who does it, when it was done, where it is done, and how it is done.

Data entry instructions. The purpose of these instructions is to provide complete information to keypunch or data entry operators for the input and/or verification of a specific job. A record layout should be attached along with a copy of the source document.

Remote terminal instructions. This document is used to provide operator instructions for entering specific data into a system via a remote terminal.

Remote job instructions. This document is used to provide complete instructions for a remote job entry machine operator to perform a specific job.

Program release. This document is used to release new or revised jobs or programs to the data processing operations department. It serves to notify data processing operations management of any changes that can affect computer operations.

Request for D.P. operations support. Applicable to a "walk-up" data processing environment where users bring requests for specific service.

Input/output control procedure. Specifies the detailed input and output control procedure used by a system.

Log of control procedures performed. Identifies control procedures and provides a means for logging, balancing, and verifying that control procedures were performed.

Tape library file history. Provides information about creation, usage, and retention of data retained on tape media.

Tapes to be scratched. A document used for identification and approval of tapes to be scratched.

EDP operations schedule. This document provides an identification of each job scheduled for processing. Includes an area for operator reporting against jobs scheduled so that all work performed, whether scheduled or unscheduled, can be accounted for.

Computer operations problem report. This report is prepared by the shift lead operator or supervisor to indicate any problems and action taken with respect to problems.

Operations daily report. A recap of activity for the past 24 hours is prepared by the data processing operations manager for presentation to the senior data processing official. The report highlights any major problems (or lack of them) so that data processing management is aware of all operating conditions.

INSTRUCTIONS FOR FORM:

SYSTEM OVERVIEW AND
SYSTEM FLOWCHART AND FLOWCHART NARRATIVE

DEFINITION OF EACH ELEMENT:

KEY	ELEMENT/CONTENT
NOTE:	Operational documentation under these headings should be the same as technical documentation and functional design specification.
	Please refer to Figure 31, Technical Documentation, for system overview.
	Please refer to Figures 7 and 8, Functional Design Specification, for system flowchart and flowchart narrative.

Figure 49
(Page 1 of 6)

JOB INSTRUCTIONS

SYSTEM NAME		PREPARED BY	DATE
PROGRAM I.D.	JOB TITLE		EST. TIME
CARD INPUT	CARD OUTPUT	PRINTER FORM	

☐ MAX TAPES ☐ MAX DISKS ☐ RESTART ☐ HOLD PARAM. USED	EST. LINES	EST. CARDS

CONSOLE OPERATING INSTRUCTIONS:

DEVICE							
SYSTEM NO.							
FILE I.D.							
DISTRIBUTION S/R							
PREVIOUS OUTPUT							
SUBSEQ. INPUT							

JOB INSTRUCTIONS

SYSTEM NAME (1)		PREPARED BY (2)	DATE (3)
PROGRAM I.D. (4)	JOB TITLE (5)		EST. TIME (6)
CARD INPUT (7)	CARD OUTPUT (8)	PRINTER FORM (9)	

[10] MAX TAPES	[11] MAX DISKS	[12] RESTART	[13] HOLD PARAM. USED	EST. LINES (14)	EST. CARDS (15)

CONSOLE OPERATING INSTRUCTIONS:

(16)

DEVICE	(17)						
SYSTEM NO.	(18)						
FILE I.D.	(19)						
DISTRIBUTION S/R	(20)						
PREVIOUS OUTPUT	(21)						
SUBSEQ. INPUT	(22)						

INSTRUCTIONS FOR FORM: JOB INSTRUCTIONS, TYPE 1

DEFINITION OF EACH ELEMENT:

KEY	ELEMENT/CONTENT
1.	System Name Name of the system in which this job is included.
2.	Prepared By Name of the person who prepared this job instruction sheet.
3.	Date Date that this sheet was prepared.
4.	Program ID Program identification code for the program that this sheet documents.
5.	Job Title Name of the processing stream that this program is a step in.
6.	Est. Time Approximate estimated running time for this job step.
7.	Card Input If card input is required, identifies the type of input.
8.	Card Output If card output is expected, identifies the type of output.
9.	Printer Form Describes the printer form to be used for printed output.
10.	Max. Tapes The maximum number of tape devices required to execute this job step.

INSTRUCTIONS FOR FORM: JOB INSTRUCTIONS, TYPE 1
Continued

DEFINITION OF EACH ELEMENT:

KEY	ELEMENT/CONTENT
11.	Max. Disks The maximum number of disk devices required to execute this job step.
12.	Restart Indicates whether this program has a restart capability (Y or N). If Y, restart procedures should be included.
13.	Hold Param. Used Y indicates that files are being locked for exclusive use by this job step. If Y, documentation should indicate which files are held.
14.	Est. Lines Estimated number of print lines expected from this job step. If variable, express a range (low-high).
15.	Est. Cards If card output is expected, estimate the number of cards required. If variable, express as a range (low-high).
16.	Console Operating Instructions Explains all setup, control, and console-response requirements for the operator's use.
17.	Device Identifies the physical device (if fixed) used to accommodate this file.
18.	System No. Identifies the logical file assignment (SYS XXX) for this file.

INSTRUCTIONS FOR FORM: JOB INSTRUCTIONS, TYPE 1

Continued

DEFINITION OF EACH ELEMENT:

KEY	ELEMENT/CONTENT
19.	File ID File identification code as it appears in job control language listings.
20.	Distribution S/R S -- scratch this file after successful execution of this job step. R -- retain this file after successful execution of this job step.
21.	Previous Output Identifies the program, by ID, that previously processed this file in the job stream.
22.	Subseq. Input Identifies the next program, by ID, that will process this file in the job stream.

EXAMPLE

JOB INSTRUCTIONS

SYSTEM NAME		PREPARED BY	DATE
Accounts Receivable		J. Doe	9/8/XX
PROGRAM I.D.: AR035	JOB TITLE: Monthly Billing		EST. TIME: 10 Min.
CARD INPUT: Select Bills	CARD OUTPUT: ---	PRINTER FORM: 4 Part Std	

				EST. LINES	EST. CARDS
[2] MAX TAPES	[1] MAX DISKS	[N] RESTART	[N] HOLD PARAM. USED	300	-0-

CONSOLE OPERATING INSTRUCTIONS:

Enter today's date in format MMDDYY

Enter bill date in format MMDDYY

At EOJ "total bills" must equal "total A/R",

otherwise cancel the stream.

DEVICE	280	281					
SYSTEM NO.	SYS022	SYS024					
FILE I.D.	CSTMST	PDTMST					
DISTRIBUTION S/R	S	S					
PREVIOUS OUTPUT	AR030	AR015					
SUBSEQ. INPUT	AR040	-----					

Figure 50
(Page 1 of 7)

JOB INSTRUCTIONS

SYSTEM: ____________________

JOB NAME |_|_|_|_|_|_|_|_|_| ____________________ DATE/INIT. __________

STEPS IN JOB __________ NORMAL RUN TIME __________ ☐ TEST ☐ PRODUCTION JCL COUNT __________ PAGE _____ OF _____

CARD INPUT / OUTPUT

STEP	FROM	IDENTIFICATION	I/O	DISPOSITION

PRINTER

CONTROL TAPE __________ PAPER FORM __________

NO. OF COPIES __________

DISK INPUT / OUTPUT

STEP	FROM	NAME	SERIAL	UNIT	I/O	S	D	DISPOSITION

RECOVERY

STEP NUMBERS	RESTART POINT	ROUTINE NO.

TAPE INPUT / OUTPUT

STEP	FROM	LABEL DESCRIPTION	LABEL I.D.	UNIT	I/O	S	D	DISP.

SPECIAL INSTRUCTIONS:

JOB INSTRUCTIONS

SYSTEM: ______ (1)

JOB NAME ______ (2)

DATE/INIT. ______ (5)

STEPS IN JOB ______ (3)

NORMAL RUN TIME ______ (4)

☐ TEST
☐ PRODUCTION (6)

JCL COUNT ______ (7)

PAGE ______ OF ______ (8)

CARD INPUT / OUTPUT

STEP	FROM	IDENTIFICATION	I/O	DISPOSITION
		(9)		

PRINTER

CONTROL TAPE ______ PAPER FORM ______

NO. OF COPIES ______ (10)

DISK INPUT / OUTPUT

STEP	FROM	NAME	SERIAL	UNIT	I/O	S	D	DISPOSITION
		(12)						

RECOVERY

STEP NUMBERS	RESTART POINT	ROUTINE NO.
(13)		

TAPE INPUT / OUTPUT

STEP	FROM	LABEL DESCRIPTION	LABEL I.D.	UNIT	I/O	S	D	DISP.
		(11)						

SPECIAL INSTRUCTIONS: (14)

(15)

INSTRUCTIONS FOR FORM: JOB INSTRUCTIONS, TYPE 2

DEFINITION OF EACH ELEMENT:

KEY	ELEMENT/CONTENT
1.	System The system name.
2.	Job Name The designation of the job.
3.	Steps in Job Specifies the number of steps in the job stream.
4.	Normal Run Time The normal or expected run time for the job.
5.	Date/Initials The effective date of the operating instruction and the initials of the manager of operations.
6.	Test/Production A check mark to designate the job as either a systems test or a production job.
7.	JCL Count The total number of job control statements, where applicable, for the job.
8.	Page This page number and the total pages in this job instruction.

INSTRUCTIONS FOR FORM: JOB INSTRUCTIONS, TYPE 2
Continued

DEFINITION OF EACH ELEMENT:

KEY	ELEMENT/CONTENT
9.	Card Input/Output

An enumeration of the card files used by the job, including:

The step in which they occur.

From where they are obtained.

Identification of the file.

Whether they are input or output.

The disposition of the file after processing.

10. Printer

Specifies the paper form, number of copies, and control tape to be used in any printed output from the job.

11. Tape Input/Output

Describes the tape files used by the job, including:

The job step in which they occur.

From where they are obtained.

The tape label description.

The tape label I.D.

The physical unit they are mounted on.

Whether they are input or output.

An "x" indication if they are to be saved (s).

An "x" indication if they are to be dated (d).

The disposition of the file after processing.

INSTRUCTIONS FOR FORM: JOB INSTRUCTIONS, TYPE 2
Continued

DEFINITION OF EACH ELEMENT:

KEY	**ELEMENT/CONTENT**
12.	Disk Input/Output

Describes the disk files used by the job, including:

The job step in which they occur.

From where they are obtained.

The file name if applicable.

The disk serial number.

The physical unit they are to be mounted on.

Whether they are input or output, if applicable.

An "x" indication if they are to be saved (s).

An "x" indication if they are to be dated (d).

The disposition of each file after processing.

13. Recovery

Specifies the restart point and recovery routine number for listed steps to be followed in case of step termination due to equipment malfunction.

14. Special Instructions

Any special instructions to be followed by an operator during the job.

15. Operations Flowchart

Flowchart of the major steps in the job flow within operations (to be attached on a separate page).

Figure 50
(Page 6 of 7)

EXAMPLE

JOB INSTRUCTIONS

SYSTEM: FINANCIAL SYSTEM DAILY

JOB NAME F S U D

DATE/INIT. 2/19/XX

STEPS IN JOB 24

NORMAL RUN TIME 4 hours

☐ TEST
☒ PRODUCTION

JCL COUNT 208 PAGE 1 OF 1

CARD INPUT / OUTPUT

STEP	FROM	IDENTIFICATION	I/O	DISPOSITION
1	K.P.	O.U. Control Cards	1	With Exec Deck
5	K.P.	Daily Issues Cards	1	Library
8	K.P.	Valid Sec # etc.	1	With Exec Deck
13	K.P.	Listing Request	1	With Exec Deck

PRINTER

CONTROL TAPE slave PAPER FORM std.

NO. OF COPIES 4

DISK INPUT / OUTPUT

STEP	FROM	NAME	SERIAL	UNIT	I/O	S	D	DISPOSITION
1-24	Lib.	FSUD07F/F1	222222	231	I/O			Lib.

RECOVERY

STEP NUMBERS	RESTART POINT	ROUTINE NO.

TAPE INPUT / OUTPUT

STEP	FROM	LABEL DESCRIPTION	LABEL I.D.	UNIT	I/O	S	D	DISP.
16	LIB	A/P Distribution	APW03	180	1			Library
19	LIB	Issues to FSD01	FSD01	181	0	X	X	FSD01
23	LIB	Daily Issues by Acct	FSUD61	180	0	X	X	LIB-ISD09
24	LIB	Issues Daily MTD	SUD62	180	1			LIB
24	LIB	Issues Daily MTD	SUD62	181	0	X	X	LIB

SPECIAL INSTRUCTIONS:

EXAMPLE

Figure 50
(Page 7 of 7)

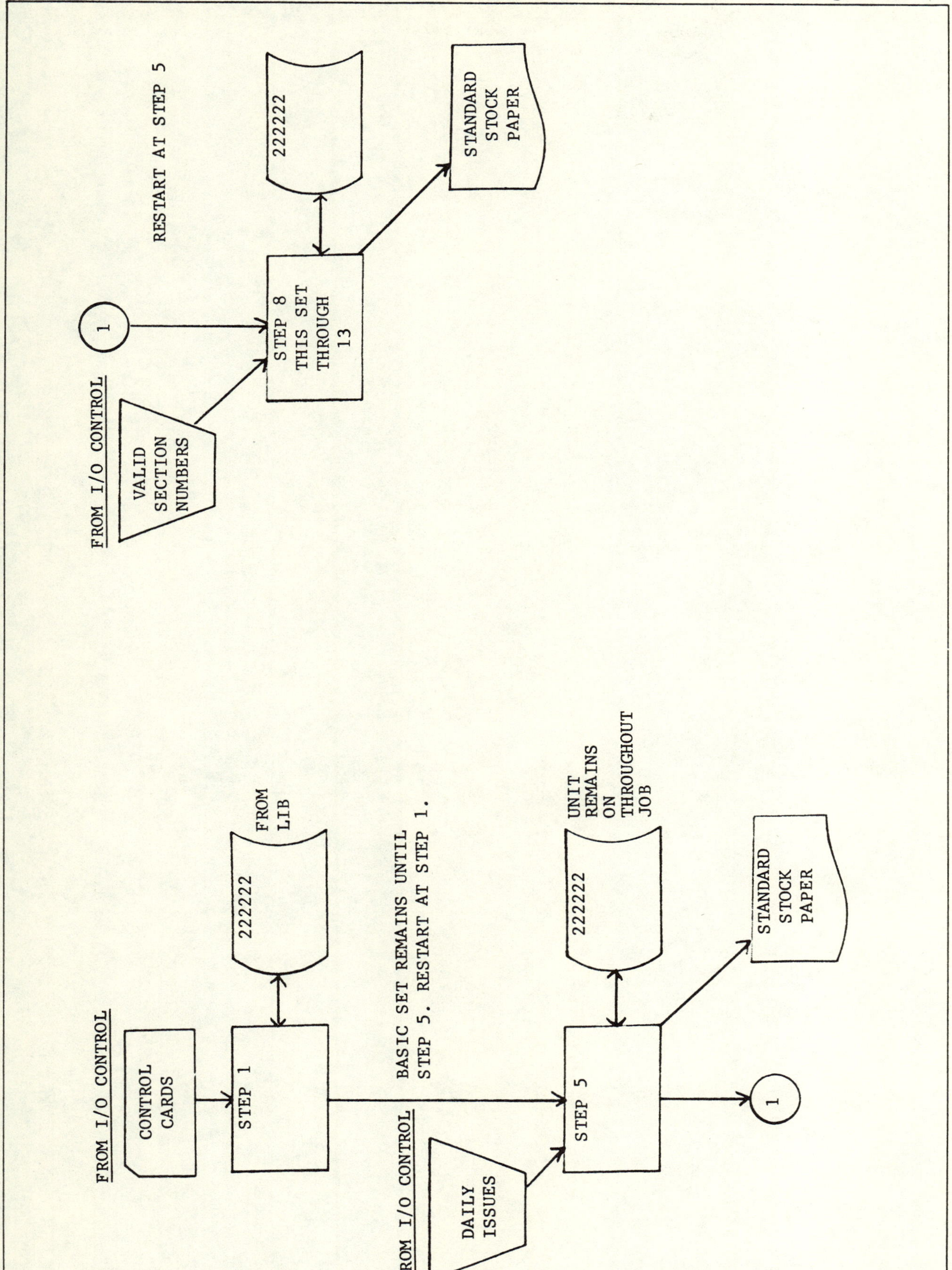

INSTRUCTIONS FOR FORM:

JOB CONTROL LISTING

DEFINITION OF EACH ELEMENT:

KEY	ELEMENT/CONTENT

NOTE: Operational documentation under this heading should be the same as technical documentation.

Please refer to Figure 41, Technical Documentation.

Figure 52
(Page 1 of 4)

CONSOLE MESSAGE LISTING

PREPARED BY: ______________________ PAGE ____ OF ____ PAGES

DATE: ______________ JOB NUMBER, NAME: ______________________ PROGRAM NUMBER: __________

MESSAGE	REASON	ACTION

Figure 52
(Page 2 of 4)

CONSOLE MESSAGE LISTING

PREPARED BY: (1) ____________________ PAGE (2) ____ OF ____ PAGES

DATE: (3) ____________ JOB NUMBER, NAME: (4) ____________ PROGRAM NUMBER: (5) ____________

MESSAGE (6)	REASON (7)	ACTION (8)

INSTRUCTIONS FOR FORM: CONSOLE MESSAGE LISTING

DEFINITION OF EACH ELEMENT:

KEY	ELEMENT/CONTENT
1.	Prepared By Name of the person who prepared the listing.
2.	Page Indicate the page sequence and total number, for example, 2 of 5.
3.	Date Date the console message listing was prepared.
4.	Job Number, Name Number and name of the job to which the listing applies.
5.	Program Number Number of the program for which the listing applies.
6.	Message List all the messages.
7.	Reason Briefly describe situation which causes the message.
8.	Action Indicate action operator should take in each case.

Figure 52
(Page 4 of 4)

EXAMPLE

CONSOLE MESSAGE LISTING

PREPARED BY: T. Roosevelt   PAGE 1 OF 1 PAGES

DATE: 01/23/XX   JOB NUMBER, NAME: Issues Validation   PROGRAM NUMBER: INVBA

MESSAGE	REASON	ACTION
Mount Tapes for INVBA	Termination of previous step	Mount the tapes as directed on the job operating instructions.
Enter Date	Program call for date comparison	Type in Date. "MMDDYY"
Weekly Listing	Optional Listing	Type "Yes" if job operating instructions indicate the list is required this date. Type "No" if no listing is required or if neither is specified.

Figure 53
(Page 1 of 4)

INPUT/OUTPUT SCHEDULE

DATE PREPARED: ____________

SYSTEM NAME: ____________

PREPARED BY: ____________

PROCESS	ESTIMATED PROCESSING TIME	CYCLE	DUE IN		DUE OUT	
			DAY	TIME	DAY	TIME

INPUT/OUTPUT SCHEDULE

DATE PREPARED: ______ (1)

SYSTEM NAME: ______ (2)

PREPARED BY: ______ (3)

PROCESS	ESTIMATED PROCESSING TIME	CYCLE	DUE IN		DUE OUT	
			DAY	TIME	DAY	TIME
(4)	(5)	(6)	(7)	(8)	(9)	(10)

INSTRUCTIONS FOR FORM: INPUT/OUTPUT SCHEDULE

DEFINITION OF EACH ELEMENT:

KEY	ELEMENT/CONTENT
1.	Date Prepared The date when the schedule was prepared.
2.	System Name Name of the application.
3.	Prepared By The person who prepared the schedule.
4.	Process Specifies the activity, program, job, data conversion, communications, or other activity.
5.	Estimated Processing Time Time required to complete the process.
6.	Cycle The period in which the process is normally repeated (daily, weekly, and so on).
7.	Due In--Day Identifies the day of the week or day of the month the data are available for processing.
8.	Due In--Time The hour of the day the data are available for processing.
9.	Due Out--Day The day of the week or day of the month the processing has been scheduled to be completed.
10.	Due Out--Time The hour of the day the processing has been scheduled to be completed.

EXAMPLE

INPUT/OUTPUT SCHEDULE

DATE PREPARED: 2/20/XX

SYSTEM NAME: Payroll

PREPARED BY: R. Johnson

PROCESS	ESTIMATED PROCESSING TIME	CYCLE	DUE IN		DUE OUT	
			DAY	TIME	DAY	TIME
User Cut-off		Daily		12 a.m.	-	-
Data Entry Cut-off	4 Hours	Daily		4 p.m.	-	8 p.m.
Pay 642	30 Min.	Weekly	Thurs.	9 a.m.	Thurs.	2 p.m.
Pay 415	60 Min.	Daily	-	11 a.m.	-	4 p.m.
Pay 502	45 Min.	Monthly	1st Mon.	10 a.m.	1st Wed.	8 p.m.

CLERICAL DESK INSTRUCTIONS

DATE PREPARED: ______________

SYSTEM NAME: ______________

PREPARED BY: ______________

TITLE OF INSTRUCTION	INSTRUCTION NO.	EFFECTIVE DATE	PAGE ______ OF ______

FREQUENCY		FORMS	VOLUME:
☐ Daily	☐ Monthly	______	______
☐ Weekly	☐ Quarterly	______	______
☐ Bi-Weekly	☐ Annual	______	______
☐ Semi-Mo.	☐ Other:	______	______

BRIEF DESCRIPTION

STEPS:

NO.	ACTION

CLERICAL DESK INSTRUCTIONS

DATE PREPARED: ______ ⑴

SYSTEM NAME: ______ ⑵

PREPARED BY: ______ ⑶

TITLE OF INSTRUCTION	INSTRUCTION NO.	EFFECTIVE DATE	PAGE ____ OF ____ (7)
(4)	(5)	(6)	

FREQUENCY (8)

- ☐ Daily
- ☐ Weekly
- ☐ Bi-Weekly
- ☐ Semi-Mo.
- ☐ Monthly
- ☐ Quarterly
- ☐ Annual
- ☐ Other:

FORMS (9)

VOLUME: (10)

BRIEF DESCRIPTION

(11)

STEPS:

NO.	ACTION
(12)	

INSTRUCTIONS FOR FORM: CLERICAL DESK INSTRUCTIONS

DEFINITION OF EACH ELEMENT:

KEY	ELEMENT/CONTENT
1.	Date Prepared Date instruction is prepared.
2.	System Name Name assigned to the process.
3.	Prepared By Person who prepared the instruction.
4.	Title of Instruction Specific name of this instruction.
5.	Instruction Number Number assigned to the instruction.
6.	Effective Date Date when instructions become effective.
7.	Page Page number, and total, for instance, 1 of 3.
8.	Frequency Specifies how often the activity is performed.
9.	Forms List of all forms (by number and name) referred to in this instruction.
10.	Volume Estimate of the quantity of each form used during the period specified under Frequency (or some other specified time)--for example, 75/week.

INSTRUCTIONS FOR FORM: CLERICAL DESK INSTRUCTIONS--Continued

DEFINITION OF EACH ELEMENT:

KEY	ELEMENT/CONTENT
11.	Brief Description An overview of the purpose and intent of the activity described by the instruction. Includes what is done, who does it, when it is done, and where it is done.
12.	Steps Identifies the action taken in each step of the activity.

EXAMPLE

CLERICAL DESK INSTRUCTIONS

DATE PREPARED: 5/20/XX

SYSTEM NAME: Payroll

PREPARED BY: R. Johnson

TITLE OF INSTRUCTION	INSTRUCTION NO.	EFFECTIVE DATE	PAGE 1 OF 1
Balancing Payroll Input Data	P-106	9/2/XX	

FREQUENCY

- [ ] Daily
- [x] Weekly
- [ ] Bi-Weekly
- [ ] Semi-Mo.
- [ ] Monthly
- [ ] Quarterly
- [ ] Annual
- [ ] Other:

FORMS	VOLUME:
Employee Time Sheets	75/week
Department Control Log	N/A

BRIEF DESCRIPTION

The purpose of this activity is to provide a control total so that the Operations Section can be sure that all Employee Status Forms were processed. The Payroll Clerk in each department does this each Monday morning before they mail the Employee Status Forms in.

STEPS:

NO.	ACTION
1	Obtain all Employee Time Sheets processed during the day.
2	Check Time Sheets to ensure that there is one sheet for each employee who worked during the day.
3	Run adding machine tape on Hours Worked and secure total.
4	Record "Hours" Total in Department Control Log, Date, and initial.
5	Attach adding machine tape to Employee Time Sheets.
6	Address package to Computer Operations Section.
7	Place in "out" mailbox for pickup.

Figure 55
(Page 1 of 6)

DATA ENTRY INSTRUCTIONS

DATE PREPARED: ____________________

SYSTEM NAME: ____________________

PREPARED BY: ____________________

PROCEDURE NAME	FREQUENCY: ☐ DAILY ☐ MONTH ☐ WEEKLY ☐ OTHER	EFFECTIVE DATE	JOB NUMBER
CARD/FORMAT NAME	FORMAT NUMBER	CARD CUT ☐ RIGHT ☐ LEFT ☐ STRIPE	CARD COLOR

SOURCE DOCUMENT	SOURCE DEPARTMENT	PRINT ☐ YES ☐ NO	PAGE OF
DISPOSITION OF CARDS	DISPOSITION OF SOURCE DOCUMENT	VERIFY: ☐ YES ☐ NO	CHARGE DEPT.

COLUMNS		NO. OF Cols.	CODE	FIELD NAME	SPECIAL INSTRUCTIONS
FROM	THRU				

CODES = Duplicate, Punch, Skip, Right or Left Shift, Zero or Blank Padding, Verify

DATA ENTRY INSTRUCTIONS

DATE PREPARED: (1) ____________________

SYSTEM NAME: (2) ____________________

PREPARED BY: (3) ____________________

PROCEDURE NAME (4)	FREQUENCY: (5) ☐ DAILY ☐ MONTH ☐ WEEKLY ☐ OTHER	EFFECTIVE DATE (6)	JOB NUMBER (7)
CARD/FORMAT NAME (8)	FORMAT NUMBER (9)	CARD CUT ☐ RIGHT ☐ LEFT ☐ STRIPE (10)	CARD COLOR (11)
SOURCE DOCUMENT (12)	SOURCE DEPARTMENT (13)	PRINT (14) ☐ YES ☐ NO	PAGE (15) OF
DISPOSITION OF CARDS (16)	DISPOSITION OF SOURCE DOCUMENT (17)	VERIFY: ☐ YES ☐ NO (18)	CHARGE DEPT. (19)

COLUMNS		NO. OF Cols.	CODE	FIELD NAME	SPECIAL INSTRUCTIONS
FROM	THRU				
(20)		(21)	(22)	(23)	(24)

CODES = Duplicate, Punch, Skip, Right or Left Shift, Zero or Blank Padding, Verify

INSTRUCTIONS FOR FORM: DATA ENTRY INSTRUCTIONS

DEFINITION OF EACH ELEMENT:

KEY	ELEMENT/CONTENT
1.	Date Prepared Date this instruction is prepared.
2.	System Name Name assigned to the system.
3.	Prepared By The person who prepared the data entry instructions.
4.	Procedure Name The name of this data entry job.
5.	Frequency Indicates how often this job is performed.
6.	Effective Date The date the instruction becomes effective.
7.	Job Number Number assigned to the data entry instructions.
8.	Card/Format Name Name of card form required (if applicable), or format name.
9.	Format Number Number of format required, or card form (if applicable).
10.	Card Cut Indicates top right corner, and/or presence of a strip (if applicable).

INSTRUCTIONS FOR FORM: DATA ENTRY INSTRUCTIONS--Continued

DEFINITION OF EACH ELEMENT:

KEY	ELEMENT/CONTENT
11.	Card Color Indicates color: manila, a solid color, or a specific color strip (if applicable).
12.	Source Document Name and form number of document, also identifies scheduled input date.
13.	Source Department The department supplying the source document.
14.	Print Indicates whether printing is required on the punched card.
15.	Page Indicates this page number, followed by total number of pages in the procedure.
16.	Disposition of Cards File cabinet or other appropriate designation.
17.	Disposition of Source Document Department or job position of person to receive source material after data entry.
18.	Verify Indicates whether any verification is to be performed.
19.	Charge Department The department or account number charged for this job.

INSTRUCTIONS FOR FORM: DATA ENTRY INSTRUCTIONS--Continued

DEFINITION OF EACH ELEMENT:

KEY	ELEMENT/CONTENT
20.	Columns Beginning and ending columns for a field. In this section, all 80 columns must be accounted for, in straight numerical sequence.
21.	Number of Columns The total number of columns in the field.
22.	Code Action to be performed in keypunch. For example: a. Duplicate b. Punch c. Skip d. Right or Left Shift e. Zero or Blank Padding f. Verify
23.	Field Name The field identification.
24.	Special Instructions Identifies contents of the field, i.e., alphabetic, numeric or combination, always present, optional, or blank, dollar and cents or whole dollars, right- or left-justified. Also identifies whether Fixed or Variable.

EXAMPLE

DATA ENTRY INSTRUCTIONS

DATE PREPARED 7/22/XX

SYSTEM NAME: Inventory

PREPARED BY: W. Osswald

PROCEDURE NAME Material Issues	FREQUENCY: [x] DAILY [ ] MONTH [ ] WEEKLY [ ] OTHER	EFFECTIVE DATE 9/16/XX	JOB NUMBER DV-104
CARD/FORMAT NAME Inventory Issues	FORMAT NUMBER I-101	CARD CUT [ ] RIGHT [ ] LEFT [ ] STRIPE N/A	CARD COLOR N/A
SOURCE DOCUMENT Stores Issues Form	SOURCE DEPARTMENT Warehouse	PRINT N/A [ ] YES [ ] NO	PAGE 1 OF 1
DISPOSITION OF CARDS N/A	DISPOSITION OF SOURCE DOCUMENT Return to Warehouse	VERIFY: [x] YES [ ] NO	CHARGE DEPT.

COLUMNS FROM	COLUMNS THRU	NO. OF Cols.	CODE	FIELD NAME	SPECIAL INSTRUCTIONS
1	6	6	P, RS, Z, V	Quantity	Numeric
7	10	4	S		
11	16	6	P, RS, Z, V	Issue Number	Numeric
17	24	8	S		
24	40	17	P	Description	Alphabetic
41	47	7	S		
48	49	2	P, RS, Z, V	Foreman Number	Numeric
50	57	8	P, PS, Z, V	Price	Numeric
58	58	1	P, V,	Credit	
59	62	4	D, RS, Z, V	Section Number	Numeric
63	69	7	P, RS, Z, V	Account Number	Numeric
70	77	8	S		
78	80	3	P, RS, Z, V	Day	Numeric

CODES = Duplicate, Punch, Skip, Right or Left Shift, Zero or Blank Padding, Verify

REMOTE TERMINAL INSTRUCTIONS

DATE PREPARED: ____________________

SYSTEM NAME: ____________________

PREPARED BY: ____________________

PROCEDURE NAME	FREQUENCY	EFFECTIVE DATE	
	☐ DAILY ☐ MONTHLY ☐ WEEKLY ☐ OTHER		PAGE ______ OF ______

SOURCE DOCUMENT	SOURCE DEPARTMENT	DISPOSITION OF SOURCE

MESSAGE	ACTION

REMOTE TERMINAL INSTRUCTIONS

(1)
DATE PREPARED: ____________

(2)
SYSTEM NAME: ____________

(3)
PREPARED BY: ____________

PROCEDURE NAME	FREQUENCY (5)	EFFECTIVE DATE	(7)
(4)	☐ DAILY ☐ MONTHLY ☐ WEEKLY ☐ OTHER	(6)	PAGE ____ OF ____

SOURCE DOCUMENT	SOURCE DEPARTMENT	DISPOSITION OF SOURCE
(8)	(9)	(10)

MESSAGE	ACTION
(11)	(12)

SYSTEMS DOCUMENTATION MANUAL

INSTRUCTIONS FOR FORM: REMOTE TERMINAL INSTRUCTIONS

DEFINITION OF EACH ELEMENT:

KEY	ELEMENT/CONTENT
1.	Date Prepared Date the form is completed.
2.	System Name Name assigned to the application.
3.	Prepared By The person who prepared the form.
4.	Procedure Name Name given to the procedure.
5.	Frequency The frequency of the procedure.
6.	Effective Date The date the instructions become effective.
7.	Page Number Page number of this instruction.
8.	Source Document The source document from which data are transcribed.
9.	Source Department The department creating the source document.
10.	Disposition of Source Document Location of the source documents after usage.

INSTRUCTIONS FOR FORM: REMOTE TERMINAL INSTRUCTIONS--Continued

DEFINITION OF EACH ELEMENT:

KEY	ELEMENT/CONTENT
11.	Message Message shown at the remote terminal that requires response from an operator.
12.	Action The proper response for an operator to make to a message.

EXAMPLE

REMOTE TERMINAL INSTRUCTIONS

DATE PREPARED: 7/22/XX

SYSTEM NAME: Inventory 824

PREPARED BY: W. Osswald

PROCEDURE NAME	FREQUENCY	EFFECTIVE DATE	
Material Receipts	[x] DAILY [ ] MONTHLY [ ] WEEKLY [ ] OTHER	9/16/XX	PAGE 1 OF 1

SOURCE DOCUMENT	SOURCE DEPARTMENT	DISPOSITION OF SOURCE
Receiving Document	Receiving	Return to Receiving

MESSAGE	ACTION
Enter:	
1. Purchase Order Number = (7 pos.)	From receiving document
2. Product Number = (8 pos.)	As noted on receiving document. Only enter items verified by Checking Department.
3. Quantity (6 pos.)	As noted by Checking Department.
	Repeat steps 2 and 3 for additional products.
	Verify product name displayed on screen against name on receiving document.

REMOTE JOB INSTRUCTIONS

DATE PREPARED: ____________________

SYSTEM NAME: ____________________

PREPARED BY: ____________________

PROCEDURE NAME	ESTIMATED TOTAL MACHINE TIME	FREQUENCY: ☐ DAILY ☐ WEEKLY ☐ MONTHLY ☐ ______	EFFECTIVE	JOB NUMBER PAGE ___ OF ___

CARDS – TITLE & FORM NUMBER	I/O	SOURCE	ESTIMATED VOLUME	OUTPUT
				☐ REPORT
				☐ SUMMARY
				☐ CARD FILE
				☐ LISTING
				☐ CARD DECK

OUTPUT TITLE	OUTPUT NUMBER	NO. OF COPIES	RECIPIENT
			1 ______
			2 ______
			3 ______
			4 ______

STEP NO.	PROCEDURAL DESCRIPTION

CHECK-OUT METHOD

Figure 57
(Page 2 of 6)

REMOTE JOB INSTRUCTIONS

DATE PREPARED: (1) ____________________

SYSTEM NAME: (2) ____________________

PREPARED BY: (3) ____________________

PROCEDURE NAME	ESTIMATED TOTAL MACHINE TIME	FREQUENCY:	EFFECTIVE	JOB NUMBER
(4)	(5)	☐ DAILY (6) ☐ WEEKLY ☐ MONTHLY ☐ ______	(7)	(8) PAGE (9) OF ___

CARDS – TITLE & FORM NUMBER	I/O	SOURCE	ESTIMATED VOLUME	OUTPUT
(10)	(11)	(12)	(13)	☐ REPORT ☐ SUMMARY ☐ CARD FILE ☐ LISTING ☐ CARD DECK (14)

OUTPUT TITLE	OUTPUT NUMBER	NO. OF COPIES	RECIPIENT
(15)	(16)	(17)	(18) 1 ______ 2 ______ 3 ______ 4 ______

STEP NO.	PROCEDURAL DESCRIPTION
(19)	(20)

CHECK-OUT METHOD

(21)

INSTRUCTIONS FOR FORM: REMOTE JOB INSTRUCTIONS

DEFINITION OF EACH ELEMENT:

KEY	ELEMENT/CONTENT
1.	Date Prepared Identifies the date this sheet is prepared.
2.	System Name Name assigned to the application.
3.	Prepared By Identifies the person who prepared the Instruction.
4.	Procedure Name Identifies the name of this job.
5.	Estimated Total Machine Time Indicates estimate of total time for all steps.
6.	Frequency Identifies how often the procedure is performed.
7.	Effective Date Identifies the date the procedure is performed.
8.	Job Number Identifies the number assigned to the operation.
9.	Page Indicate current page number followed by total number of pages in the instruction.
10.	Cards--Title and Form Number Indicates the name and form number of the required cards.

INSTRUCTIONS FOR FORM: REMOTE JOB INSTRUCTIONS--Continued

DEFINITION OF EACH ELEMENT:

KEY	ELEMENT/CONTENT
11.	I/O Indicates whether this card is an input or output to the procedure.
12.	Source Identifies the department supplying the cards.
13.	Estimated Volume Identifies the approximate number of cards used in the procedure.
14.	Output Indicates the form of the job output.
15.	Output Title Identifies name of the printed or other output.
16.	Output Number Indicates the report number or other identification associated with the product of the job.
17.	Number of Copies Identifies the number of copies of printed outputs.
18.	Recipient Identifies the department or job position receiving printed material from the job.
19.	Step Number Indicates the sequentially numbered step in the procedure.

INSTRUCTIONS FOR FORM: REMOTE JOB INSTRUCTIONS--Continued

DEFINITION OF EACH ELEMENT:

KEY	ELEMENT/CONTENT
20.	Procedural Description Identifies the specific actions required to perform this step.
21.	Check-Out Method Explains how the output of the job is to be checked for accuracy.

EXAMPLE

REMOTE JOB INSTRUCTIONS

DATE PREPARED: 9/6/XX

SYSTEM NAME: GENERAL LEDGER

PREPARED BY: AWP

PROCEDURE NAME	ESTIMATED TOTAL MACHINE TIME	FREQUENCY:	EFFECTIVE	JOB NUMBER
UPDATE MONTHLY JOURNAL	10 min.	☐ DAILY ☐ WEEKLY ☒ MONTHLY ☐ ______	B002AYGL (Step 1)	B003AYGL PAGE 1 OF 12

CARDS – TITLE & FORM NUMBER	I/O	SOURCE	ESTIMATED VOLUME	OUTPUT
Control Cards (See Step 2, 3)	I			☐ REPORT
Data Cards (See Step 2)	I	Data Control		☐ SUMMARY
				☐ CARD FILE
				☒ LISTING
				☐ CARD DECK

OUTPUT TITLE	OUTPUT NUMBER	NO. OF COPIES	RECIPIENT
Monthly Journal Input Error Listing	ILGL 6	1	1 Accounting--Herb Smith 2 3 4

STEP NO.	PROCEDURAL DESCRIPTION
1	If Job B002AYGL was not Required, this Job is Run After Job B001AYGL.
2	Control and Data Cards are Placed Between "11 EXEC 203" and "/*".
3	Control Card Format: Pos 1- 4 "GLR1" (Constant).
	10-15 MMDDYY Day of Processing.
	16-19 MMYY Month being Processed
	(Usually Prior Month).
	23-24 Asterisks "**" (Constant).
	57-62 MMDDYY Day of Processing.
	63-68 MMDDYY Day of Processing.
	69-74 MMDDYY Day of Processing.
	75-80 MMDDYY Day of Processing.

CHECK-OUT METHOD

Figure 58
(Page 1 of 6)

PROGRAM RELEASE

DATE:

TO: DATA PROCESSING OPERATIONS	FROM:

JOB NUMBER	JOB NAME	PROGRAM NUMBER

NATURE OF CHANGE

☐ NEW INSTALLATION ☐ JCL ☐ CHANGE PROGRAM ☐ DOCUMENTATION ☐ SUSPEND ☐ COPY SOURCE PROD. TO TEST

EFFECTIVE DATE:	SUPERSEDES:

PURPOSE:

SPECIAL INSTRUCTIONS:

ENCLOSURES: ☐ JCL REPLACEMENT ☐ JCL MODIFICATION ☐ JCL LISTINGS
☐ DOCUMENTATION MODIFICATIONS ☐ OTHER (Described above)

PREPARED BY: APPROVED BY:

Programmer	Date	Manager, Systems	Date

CONCURRED BY: ACCEPTED BY:

Analyst	Date	Manager, Operations	Date

PROGRAM RELEASE

DATE: (1)

TO: DATA PROCESSING OPERATIONS

FROM: (2)

JOB NUMBER (3) | JOB NAME (4) | PROGRAM NUMBER (5)

NATURE OF CHANGE

☐ NEW INSTALLATION (6)
☐ JCL
☐ CHANGE PROGRAM
☐ DOCUMENTATION (7)
☐ SUSPEND (8)
☐ COPY SOURCE PROD. TO TEST (9)

EFFECTIVE DATE: (10)

SUPERSEDES: (11)

PURPOSE: (12)

SPECIAL INSTRUCTIONS: (13)

ENCLOSURES: (14)
☐ JCL REPLACEMENT
☐ JCL MODIFICATION
☐ JCL LISTINGS
☐ DOCUMENTATION MODIFICATIONS
☐ OTHER (Described above)

PREPARED BY: (15)

Programmer ________ Date ________

APPROVED BY: (17)

Manager, Systems ________ Date ________

CONCURRED BY: (16)

Analyst ________ Date ________

ACCEPTED BY: (18)

Manager, Operations ________ Date ________

INSTRUCTIONS FOR FORM: PROGRAM RELEASE

DEFINITION OF EACH ELEMENT:

KEY **ELEMENT/CONTENT**

1. Date

   Date the document was prepared.

2. From

   Name of person submitting the program release.

3. Job Number

   Number of the processing stream affected.

4. Job Name

   Name of the processing stream affected by the release.

5. Program Number

   Program identification code for the program that this sheet releases. If several programs are involved, they should be noted under Special Instructions.

6. New Installation

   Identifies if a new program is being installed.

7. Nature of Change

   Identifies the extent of changes:

   JCL--Job control language statements

   Program

   Documentation

   Any one, or a combination of these, may be affected.

8. Suspend

   Identifies if a current processing stream is to be suspended from operation.

INSTRUCTIONS FOR FORM: PROGRAM RELEASE--Continued

DEFINITION OF EACH ELEMENT:

KEY	ELEMENT/CONTENT
9.	Copy Source Production to Test Identifies if source code is to be copied for subsequent modification. This is normally done before changes are made to existing programs.
10.	Effective Date Date the release is to become effective.
11.	Supersedes Indicates previous release date for this job that this release supersedes.
12.	Purpose Brief description of the reason for the change effected by this release.
13.	Special Instructions Identifies any unique processing steps that data processing operations personnel should be aware of. Transfers of test library source and object code to production library would also be indicated.
14.	Enclosures Identification of documentation provided with this release.
15.	Prepared By Name of the programmer responsible for the release. Includes date of preparation.
16.	Concurred By Name of the project analyst responsible for the changes made. Includes date of concurrence.

INSTRUCTIONS FOR FORM: PROGRAM RELEASE--Continued

DEFINITION OF EACH ELEMENT:

KEY	ELEMENT/CONTENT
17.	Approved By Name of systems manager responsible for assuring that testing of programs is satisfactorily performed. Includes date of approval.
18.	Accepted By Name of data processing operations manager who has verified that proper documentation and instructions are provided. Includes date of acceptance.

EXAMPLE

PROGRAM RELEASE

DATE: 4/7/XX

TO: DATA PROCESSING OPERATIONS	FROM: W. Holman

JOB NUMBER 3224	JOB NAME PO Status	PROGRAM NUMBER

NATURE OF CHANGE

☐ NEW INSTALLATION	☒ JCL	☒ CHANGE PROGRAM	☒ DOCUMENTATION	☐ SUSPEND	☐ COPY SOURCE PROD. TO TEST

EFFECTIVE DATE:	SUPERSEDES:

PURPOSE: Changing Report Formats
Changing Number of Copies From 5 to 3

SPECIAL INSTRUCTIONS:

1 - Copy from Testlib to Prodlib:

Librarian		Testgo
NPO210WH	-FTF2-	NPO210
NPO230WH	-XPTF-	NPO230

2 - Replace 5th card from the back of the JCL's with the attached card--changing number of copies.

3 - Replace distribution of report.

ENCLOSURES: ☒ JCL REPLACEMENT ☐ JCL MODIFICATION ☐ JCL LISTINGS
☒ DOCUMENTATION MODIFICATIONS ☐ OTHER (Described above)

PREPARED BY:		APPROVED BY:	
Walter Holman	4/7/XX	T. Noshman	4/7/XX
Programmer	Date	Manager, Systems	Date

CONCURRED BY:		ACCEPTED BY:	
R. Verduin	4/7/XX	W. Marino	4/8/XX
Analyst	Date	Manager, Operations	Date

Figure 59
(Page 1 of 4)

REQUEST FOR DATA PROCESSING OPERATIONS SUPPORT

TO: DATA PROCESSING OPERATIONS DATE: ____________

FROM: DEPARTMENT NO. ________ NAME: ____________ EXT.: ________

DISPOSITION

JOB NO. ____________ ☐ CALL

JOB NAME ____________ ☐ DELIVER

BATCH NO. ____________ ☐ HOLD FILE

PROCESSING REQUIRED

☐ KEYPUNCH ☐ 4300 OPERATION

☐ VERIFY ☐ XEROX

☐ ____________

4300 OPERATIONS ONLY:

EST. RUN TIME ____________

CPU TIME (MIN) ____________

TAPES REQUIRED ____________

DISKS REQUIRED ____________

NO. OF COPIES ____________

PUNCH OUT ____________

SPECIAL INSTRUCTIONS ____________

____

____

____

FOR DPO USE ONLY

SCHEDULE	TIME	DATE	OPERATIONS COMMENTS
RECEIVED			
K P COMPLETE			
COMPLETE			
4300 COMPLETE			

Figure 59
(Page 2 of 4)

REQUEST FOR DATA PROCESSING OPERATIONS SUPPORT

(1)

TO: DATA PROCESSING OPERATIONS DATE: ____________

FROM: DEPARTMENT NO. ______ (2) NAME: ______ (3) EXT.: ______

JOB NO. ______ (4)

JOB NAME ______ (5)

BATCH NO. ______ (6)

DISPOSITION (7)

☐ CALL

☐ DELIVER

☐ HOLD FILE

PROCESSING REQUIRED

☐ KEYPUNCH (8)

☐ VERIFY

☐ 4300 OPERATION

☐ XEROX

☐ ______

4300 OPERATIONS ONLY: (9)

EST. RUN TIME ______

CPU TIME (MIN) ______

TAPES REQUIRED ______

DISKS REQUIRED ______

NO. OF COPIES ______

PUNCH OUT ______

SPECIAL INSTRUCTIONS ______ (10)

FOR DPO USE ONLY (11)

SCHEDULE	TIME	DATE	OPERATIONS COMMENTS
RECEIVED			
K P COMPLETE			
COMPLETE			
4300 COMPLETE			

INSTRUCTIONS FOR FORM: REQUEST FOR DATA PROCESSING OPERATIONS SUPPORT

DEFINITION OF EACH ELEMENT:

KEY	ELEMENT/CONTENT
1.	Date Date that the support is requested.
2.	From Department number of requester.
3.	Name Name of person submitting the request for support.
4.	Job Number Number of the processing stream affected.
5.	Job Name Name of the processing stream affected.
6.	Batch Number Identification of specific data to be processed.
7.	Disposition Identification of data processing action upon completion.
8.	Processing Required Identification of specific support requested.
9.	Computer Operations Support Identification of potential running times, plus specific files and output documents to be used.
10.	Special Instructions As required.
11.	Data Processing Operations Use Identifies and logs dates, times, and operational comments pertinent to work performed.

EXAMPLE

Figure 59
(Page 4 of 4)

REQUEST FOR DATA PROCESSING OPERATIONS SUPPORT

TO: DATA PROCESSING OPERATIONS DATE: June 14, 19XX

FROM: DEPARTMENT NO. 2100 NAME: G. Smith EXT.: 293

JOB NO. XPL003

JOB NAME A/P test

BATCH NO. ____

DISPOSITION

[X] CALL

[ ] DELIVER

[ ] HOLD FILE

PROCESSING REQUIRED

[ ] KEYPUNCH

[X] 4300 OPERATION

[ ] VERIFY

[ ] XEROX

[ ] ____

4300 OPERATIONS ONLY:

EST. RUN TIME 20 min.

CPU TIME (MIN) ____

TAPES REQUIRED 2--XPL004, XPL006

DISKS REQUIRED 1--XPL010

NO. OF COPIES ____

PUNCH OUT ____

SPECIAL INSTRUCTIONS Additional scratch tape drive required

FOR DPO USE ONLY

SCHEDULE	TIME	DATE	OPERATIONS COMMENTS
RECEIVED	10:00	6/14/XX	JB
K P COMPLETE			
COMPLETE			
4300 COMPLETE	2:00	6/14/XX	JB

INPUT / OUTPUT CONTROL PROCEDURE

DATE PREPARED: ____________________

SYSTEM NAME: ____________________

SYSTEM NO.: ____________________ PREPARED BY: ____________________

JOB/	JOB/ NO.	EFFECTIVE DATE	PAGE ______ OF ______

FREQUENCY	FORMS:	TYPE I/O	FORMS:	TYPE I/O
☐ DAILY ☐ MONTHLY				
☐ WEEKLY ☐ QUARTERLY				
☐ BI-WEEKLY ☐ ANNUAL				
☐ SEMI-MO. ☐ OTHER:				

ITEM	ACTION

INPUT/OUTPUT CONTROL PROCEDURE

DATE PREPARED: ______ (1)

SYSTEM NAME: ______ (2)

SYSTEM NO.: ______ (3) PREPARED BY: ______ (4)

JOB/ (5)	JOB/ NO. (6)	EFFECTIVE DATE (7)	PAGE ___ OF ___ (8)

FREQUENCY (9)

- ☐ DAILY
- ☐ WEEKLY
- ☐ BI-WEEKLY
- ☐ SEMI-MO.
- ☐ MONTHLY
- ☐ QUARTERLY
- ☐ ANNUAL
- ☐ OTHER:

FORMS: (10)	TYPE I/O	FORMS:	TYPE I/O
	(11)		

ITEM	ACTION
(12)	(13)

INSTRUCTIONS FOR FORM: INPUT/OUTPUT CONTROL PROCEDURE

DEFINITION OF EACH ELEMENT:

KEY **ELEMENT/CONTENT**

1. Date Prepared

   Date of preparation.

2. System Name

   The name assigned to the system.

3. System Number

   The number assigned to the system.

4. Prepared By

   Analyst who prepared the procedure.

5. Job Name

   The name of the job covered by the procedure, if applicable.

6. Job Number

   The number of the job covered by the procedure, if applicable.

7. Effective Date

   The date the procedure goes into effect.

8. Page

   The page number within the procedure.

9. Frequency

   The frequency that the procedure is performed.

10. Forms

    The name of each form used with the procedure.

11. Type

    Classification of each form as input or output.

INSTRUCTIONS FOR FORM: INPUT/OUTPUT CONTROL PROCEDURE--Continued

DEFINITION OF EACH ELEMENT:

KEY	ELEMENT/CONTENT
12.	Item The name of a particular form or procedure.
13.	Action Detailed control procedures of each form or procedure identified in the "item" columns.

EXAMPLE

INPUT / OUTPUT CONTROL PROCEDURE

DATE PREPARED: 3/20/XX

SYSTEM NAME: Hourly Payroll

SYSTEM NO.: 898 PREPARED BY: E. Muskie

JOB/	JOB/ NO.	EFFECTIVE DATE	PAGE / OF
Data count verification	893	3/27/XX	PAGE 1 OF 1

FREQUENCY		FORMS:	TYPE I/O	FORMS:	TYPE I/O
[X] DAILY	[ ] MONTHLY	Console Message	I		
[ ] WEEKLY	[ ] QUARTERLY				
[ ] BI-WEEKLY	[ ] ANNUAL				
[ ] SEMI-MO.	[ ] OTHER:				

ITEM	ACTION
Input Console Control Message	1. Compare the header record total to the computer count of the number of records read. 2. If they are equal, no action is required. 3. If they are unequal, communicate with the sending location to determine the cause of the discrepancy. 4. If it is impossible to determine the cause of the discrepancy, request <u>one</u> retransmittal. 5. If there is still a discrepancy after one retransmittal of the data, then request a printout of the data and obtain assistance from Operations Manager.

LOG OF CONTROL PROCEDURES PERFORMED

DATE ____________________ SHIFT ______________ PERFORMED BY ______________________

____ FREQUENCY ☐ D ☐ W ☐ M ______ OTHER
(NAME OF PROCEDURE)

$______________________ = $______________________ ☐ OK ☐ PROBLEM - (NOTE BELOW)
(REPORT ____________) (REPORT ____________)

____ FREQUENCY ☐ D ☐ W ☐ M ______ OTHER
(NAME OF PROCEDURE)

$______________________ = $______________________ ☐ OK ☐ PROBLEM - (NOTE BELOW)
(REPORT ____________) (REPORT ____________)

____ FREQUENCY ☐ D ☐ W ☐ M ______ OTHER
(NAME OF PROCEDURE)

______________ + ______________ = ______________ ☐ OK ☐ PROBLEM - (NOTE BELOW)
(REPORT ________) (REPORT ________) (REPORT ________)

ETC.
(FORMAT AS NEEDED)

NOTE: REFER TO CONTROL PROCEDURE FOR INSTRUCTIONS. REPORT ON PROBLEM RESOLUTION BELOW.

CONTROL PROBLEM RESOLUTION: ______________________________________
NAME OF PROCEDURE

ACTION TAKEN: ____

____

____

____

(ATTACH ADDITIONAL FORM IF REQUIRED)

LOG OF CONTROL PROCEDURES PERFORMED

DATE ___(1)___ SHIFT ___(2)___ PERFORMED BY ___(3)___

___(4)___ FREQUENCY ☐ D ☐ W ☐ M ___(5)___ OTHER
(NAME OF PROCEDURE)

$______ = $______ ☐ OK ☐ PROBLEM - (NOTE BELOW)
(REPORT ______) (6) (REPORT ______)

______ FREQUENCY ☐ D ☐ W ☐ M ______ OTHER
(NAME OF PROCEDURE)

$______ = $______ ☐ OK ☐ PROBLEM - (NOTE BELOW)
(REPORT ______) (REPORT ______)

______ FREQUENCY ☐ D ☐ W ☐ M ______ OTHER
(NAME OF PROCEDURE)

______ + ______ = ______ ☐ OK ☐ PROBLEM - (NOTE BELOW)
(REPORT ______) (REPORT ______) (REPORT ______)

ETC.
(FORMAT AS NEEDED)

NOTE: REFER TO CONTROL PROCEDURE FOR INSTRUCTIONS. REPORT ON PROBLEM RESOLUTION BELOW.

CONTROL PROBLEM RESOLUTION: ______
NAME OF PROCEDURE

(7)
ACTION TAKEN: ______
______
______
______

(ATTACH ADDITIONAL FORM IF REQUIRED)

INSTRUCTIONS FOR FORM:

LOG OF CONTROL PROCEDURES PERFORMED

DEFINITION OF EACH ELEMENT:

KEY	ELEMENT/CONTENT
1.	Date Date that control procedures are performed.
2.	Shift Shift or time period that control procedures are performed.
3.	Performed By Individual performing the control procedures.
4.	Name of Procedure Name identified with the procedure. Detail instructions for performing the procedure are identified on the "Clerical Desk Instructions" document.
5.	Frequency Identifies frequency and may include date for weekly and monthly controls.
6.	Computation and Verification of Results This structure is tailored to the procedure to be followed. Reports to be used are predefined. Data (dollars, record counts, and the like, as appropriate) are extracted from reports, and added and/or compared as required. Completeness and accuracy of output are noted (check "OK"), or problems are indicated.
7.	Control Problem Resolution Any problems noted in item 6 are identified here in detail, along with corrective action taken.

EXAMPLE

LOG OF CONTROL PROCEDURES PERFORMED

DATE 3/28/XX SHIFT 1 PERFORMED BY JWT

NDA Daily File
(NAME OF PROCEDURE)

FREQUENCY ☐ D ☐ W ☐ M ______ OTHER

$ $238,963.94 (REPORT NDD092) = $ $238,963.94 (REPORT NDD805)

☑ OK ☐ PROBLEM - (NOTE BELOW)

G/L Balance Report
(NAME OF PROCEDURE)

FREQUENCY ☐ D ☐ W ☐ M ______ OTHER

$ $425,800.18 (REPORT REG050) = $ $350,176.22 (REPORT GL090)

☐ OK ☑ PROBLEM - (NOTE BELOW)

CD's Paid to Maturity
(NAME OF PROCEDURE)

FREQUENCY ☐ D ☐ W ☐ M ______ OTHER

$123,814.32 (REPORT SVW090) + $84,322.20 (REPORT SVW801) (REPRO CHECKS) = $208,136.52 (REPORT SVW801) (TOT. # OF CKS)

☑ OK ☐ PROBLEM - (NOTE BELOW)

ETC.
(FORMAT AS NEEDED)

NOTE: REFER TO CONTROL PROCEDURE FOR INSTRUCTIONS. REPORT ON PROBLEM RESOLUTION BELOW.

CONTROL PROBLEM RESOLUTION: G/L Balance Report
NAME OF PROCEDURE

ACTION TAKEN: Accounts Payable data not provided. Notified D.P operations - Jim Clark at 10:30. Possible re-run.

(ATTACH ADDITIONAL FORM IF REQUIRED)

TAPE LIBRARY FILE HISTORY

FILE NAME: ______________________ **FILE NUMBER** ______________

RETENTION CYCLE: ______________

OTHER NOTES: ______________

USED IN JOBS:

ISSUED / RETURNED

DATE CREATED OR PERIOD	TO	WHEN	RETURNED	REEL IDENTIFICATION				

TAPE LIBRARY FILE HISTORY

(1) FILE NAME: ______________________ (2) FILE NUMBER ______________

(3) RETENTION CYCLE: ______________

OTHER NOTES: ______________

(4) USED IN JOBS:

(5) ISSUED / RETURNED

DATE CREATED OR PERIOD	TO	WHEN	RETURNED	REEL IDENTIFICATION				

INSTRUCTIONS FOR FORM:

TAPE LIBRARY FILE HISTORY

DEFINITION OF EACH ELEMENT:

KEY	ELEMENT/CONTENT
1.	File Name Identifies the name of the data file contained on tape.
2.	File Number Number associated with the file.
3.	Retention Cycle Identifies the length of time that the file is to be retained before it is scratched.
4.	Used in Jobs Identifies various jobs that may use the tape file.
5.	Issued/Returned o Date Created or Period: Identification of the creation date, or the period of data that the file represents. o To: To whom (operator, programmer, or job) the tape(s) are released. Scratched tapes are also identified here. o When: Date that the tape(s) are released (or scratched). o Returned: Date that the tape(s) are returned. o Reel Identification: Specific numbers associated with each reel of tape.

EXAMPLE

TAPE LIBRARY FILE HISTORY

FILE NAME: Payroll Transactions **FILE NUMBER** PAY 020T

RETENTION CYCLE: 6 weeks

OTHER NOTES:

USED IN JOBS:
PAY010 PAY065
PAY020
PAY040

ISSUED / RETURNED

DATE CREATED OR PERIOD	TO	WHEN	RETURNED	REEL IDENTIFICATION				
10/1/XX	JAB	10/4/XX	10/5/XX	3456				
10/8/XX	JAB	10/9/XX	10/12/XX	4567	2382			
10/15/XX	CW	10/17/XX	10/18/XX	5678				
10/22/XX	JAB	10/24/XX	10/26/XX	6789				
10/29/XX	JAB	10/30/XX	11/2/XX	7890				
10/15/XX	JAB	11/2/XX	11/4/XX	5678				
11/3/XX	CW	11/4/XX	11/6/XX	8901				
11/10/XX	CW	11/11/XX	11/13/XX	9012				
10/1/XX	SCRATCH	11/13/XX	–	3456				
11/17/XX	JAB	11/18/XX	11/20/XX	3456				
11/24/XX	JAB	11/26/XX		0123				

Figure 63
(Page 1 of 4)

To: Data Processing Operations

TAPES TO BE SCRATCHED

REEL NUMBER	DATA SET / JOB NAME	CREATION DATE	COMMENTS

PREPARED BY: ______________________ DATE ______________

APPROVED BY: ______________________ DATE ______________

To: Data Processing Operations

TAPES TO BE SCRATCHED

REEL NUMBER	DATA SET / JOB NAME	CREATION DATE	COMMENTS
(1)	(2)	(3)	(4)

PREPARED BY: ______ (5) ______ DATE ______ (6) ______

APPROVED BY: ______ (7) ______ DATE ______ (8) ______

INSTRUCTIONS FOR FORM:

TAPES TO BE SCRATCHED

DEFINITION OF EACH ELEMENT:

KEY	ELEMENT/CONTENT
1.	Reel Number Number associated with the physical reel of tape.
2.	Data Set/Job Name Identifying information pertaining to data on the tape.
3.	Creation Date Date that data were written onto tape.
4.	Comments Any additional information pertaining to scratching of data on tape. May identify reason ("rerun," "as per normal retention," "test data no longer needed," and the like).
5.	Prepared By Signature of the operations person, tape librarian, or programmer releasing tape to be scratched.
6.	Date Date the form was prepared.
7.	Approved By Signature of the operations supervisor, systems analyst, or programming manager who has approved the release of tapes to be scratched.
8.	Date Date of approval.

EXAMPLE

To: Data Processing Operations

TAPES TO BE SCRATCHED

REEL NUMBER	DATA SET / JOB NAME	CREATION DATE	COMMENTS
6253	TTSI - From SVD810	6/24/XX	Normal Retention passed
4028	MOTC - From NDD806	5/13/XX	Normal Retention passed
5019	DDAP - From ODA510	6/19/XX	Normal Retention passed
3032	TTSI - From SVD810	7/23/XX	Rerun was performed

PREPARED BY: R. Rivera **DATE** 7/24/XX

APPROVED BY: G. White **DATE** 7/24/XX

Figure 64
(Page 1 of 6)

EDP OPERATIONS SCHEDULE

DATE ____________ SHIFT ________ PREPARED/**APPROVED BY**____________

JOB NO., NAME	FREQ.	INPUT CTL. PARAM.	INPUT DATE	SCHEDULED		ACTUAL				
				START	ELAPSED	START	STOP	RESULT	COMMENTS	OPER. INIT.

EDP OPERATIONS SCHEDULE

DATE ______ (1) SHIFT ______ PREPARED/APPROVED BY ______ (2)

JOB NO., NAME	FREQ.	INPUT CTL. PARAM.	INPUT DATE	SCHEDULED		ACTUAL				
				START	ELAPSED	START	STOP	RESULT	COMMENTS	OPER. INIT.
(3)	(4)	(5)	(6)	(7)		(8)		(9)	(10)	(11)

INSTRUCTIONS FOR FORM:

EDP OPERATIONS SCHEDULE

DEFINITION OF EACH ELEMENT:

KEY	ELEMENT/CONTENT
1.	Date/Shift Date and shift to which this schedule applies.
2.	Prepared/Approved By Operations supervisor, manager, or control function responsible for preparation of the schedule.
3.	Job Number, Name The identifier reference for initiation and execution of the job. Generally, jobs are listed in order of their execution.
4.	Frequency Identifies whether job is daily, weekly, and so on. Convention may be established as follows: D (Daily--If the evening schedules may vary because of variable times associated with on-line daytime processing, variable evening schedules may be identified as D1, D2, and so on). W02 (Weekly--run on Tuesday) M25 (Monthly--run on or about 25th day) Q (Quarterly) A (Annual)
5.	Input Control Parameter Any operation run codes that must be entered for proper execution of this job are noted here by an independent control or job-scheduling function as a guide to the operator. Operator will further confirm proper code usage by using operational procedure.

INSTRUCTIONS FOR FORM:

EDP OPERATIONS SCHEDULE--continued

DEFINITION OF EACH ELEMENT:

KEY	ELEMENT/CONTENT
6.	Input Date Any dates required for date sensitive jobs (for example, interest calculation, accounts-payable cash requirements) are noted here by the independent control or job-scheduling function. Operator will further confirm proper date usage by using operational procedure.
7.	Scheduled Start/Elapsed Indicates the normal expected start time and elapsed time required. The elapsed time is not intended for job termination. It is intended to make the operator aware of average running time so that excessive actual time will be noticed and investigated.
8.	Actual Start/Stop Insertion, by the operator, of the actual start and stop time for the job.
9.	Result Codified recap of whether the job was completed successfully or not. Suggested result codes are as follows: S--Successfully Completed IE--Input Error OE--Output Error PE--Program Error EF--Equipment Failure RR--Rerun When equipment maintenance is performed, or the equipment is idle, reason and time notations should also be noted in order to account for all equipment time. Suggested codes are: SM--Schedule Maintenance NM--Non-Schedule Maintenance ID--Idle

INSTRUCTIONS FOR FORM:

EDP OPERATIONS SCHEDULE--continued

DEFINITION OF EACH ELEMENT:

KEY	ELEMENT/CONTENT
10.	Comments Remarks may be inserted here by the scheduler as needed to inform the operator, or by the operator regarding the performance of the job.
11.	Operator Initials Initials of the operator responsible for execution of the job.

NOTE: A schedule of this type is readily automated by use of a records, file, or word processor, enabling jobs to be printed out according to frequency code. Test or on-request jobs would be hand-scheduled.

Any operations activity (say, file reorganization) performed which was not scheduled, or any machine time availability or downtime, would be identified under the ACTUAL heading.

EXAMPLE

EDP OPERATIONS SCHEDULE

DATE March 17, 19XX SHIFT 2 PREPARED/APPROVED BY L. Peters

JOB NO., NAME	FREQ.	INPUT CTL. PARAM.	INPUT DATE	SCHEDULED START	SCHEDULED ELAPSED	ACTUAL START	ACTUAL STOP	ACTUAL RESULT	ACTUAL COMMENTS	OPER. INIT.
NDD800	D	D	0117XX	5:00	1:30	5:17	6:50	S		JS
SVD810	D	D	0117XX	5:30	1:00	5:25	6:10	S		JS
DLEXPL	D	-	-	6:00	:30	5:50	6:30	S		JS
NDFP	D	-	-	7:00	:15	7:15	7:30	S	Do not run before completion of NDD800.	JS
SVD090	D	-	0118XX	7:15	:45	7:05	8:15	S		JS
AP040	W04	W, 4, 30	0117XX, 0124XX	8:00	:30	9:00	9:25	S		JS
NDD810	D	-	-	8:30	6:00	8:25	2:50	S	Tape input label 324 NDFP output.	JS
Test Bob R SLM003		—	-	9:00	10 min	9:30	9:32	PE	abort-file not found.	JS

Figure 65
(Page 1 of 4)

To: Manager, D.P. Operations

COMPUTER OPERATIONS
PROBLEM REPORT

DATE ____________________ SHIFT ______________ REPORTED BY ________________________

JOB NO., NAME IF APPLICABLE	TIME OF OCCURRENCE	NATURE OF PROBLEM IDENTIFY IN DETAIL, INCLUDING ACTION TAKEN

To: Manager, D.P. Operations

COMPUTER OPERATIONS
PROBLEM REPORT

DATE ______________ (1) SHIFT ______________ (2) REPORTED BY ______________ (3)

JOB NO., NAME IF APPLICABLE	TIME OF OCCURRENCE	NATURE OF PROBLEM IDENTIFY IN DETAIL, INCLUDING ACTION TAKEN
(4)	(5)	(6)

INSTRUCTIONS FOR FORM:

COMPUTER OPERATIONS PROBLEM REPORT

DEFINITION OF EACH ELEMENT:

KEY	ELEMENT/CONTENT
1.	Date Date encompassed by the report.
2.	Shift Shift, or period of time of the day, encompassed by the report.
3.	Reported By Preparer, or person responsible for reporting.
4.	Job Number, Name Specific process for which difficulty was encountered. May include problems not related to specific computer jobs, such as air conditioning problems, shortage of paper stock and the like.
5.	Time of Occurrence Time that the problem occurred.
6.	Nature of Problem Narrative in detail of the problem and corrective action taken.

EXAMPLE

To: Manager, D.P. Operations

COMPUTER OPERATIONS
PROBLEM REPORT

DATE March 24/XX SHIFT 2 REPORTED BY D. Monica

JOB NO., NAME IF APPLICABLE	TIME OF OCCURRENCE	NATURE OF PROBLEM IDENTIFY IN DETAIL, INCLUDING ACTION TAKEN
XBM 003	9:45 p.	Exceeded normal processing time. Loop on account number 1234. Called Ops. mgr. - aborted job at 10:00 p as per instructions from Ops. mgr.
Stock	11:30 p	Running low on Form 3896 - Statements

Figure 66
(Page 1 of 4)

OPERATIONS DAILY REPORT

To:

From: Data Processing Operations

PERFORMANCE FOR 8:00 PRIOR DAY TO 8:00 AM TODAY (Date) ____________________

COMMUNICATIONS	PROCESSING
☐ Systems OK	☐ All Scheduled Jobs Run
☐ Problems:	☐ Incomplete Processing:

INPUT / OUTPUT / TAPE CONTROLS	EQUIPMENT PERFORMANCE
☐ Controls in Balance	☐ All Equipment in Order
☐ Problems:	☐ Problems:

OTHER: *(Attendance, Supplies, New Production Jobs Accepted, Future Concerns, etc.)*

____

____

____

____

____

____

DATA PROCESSING MANAGER ____________ DATE ____________

OPERATIONS DAILY REPORT

To: (1)

From: Data Processing Operations

PERFORMANCE FOR 8:00 PRIOR DAY TO 8:00 AM TODAY (Date)

COMMUNICATIONS (2)	**PROCESSING** (3)
☐ Systems OK	☐ All Scheduled Jobs Run
☐ Problems:	☐ Incomplete Processing:

INPUT / OUTPUT / TAPE CONTROLS (4)	**EQUIPMENT PERFORMANCE** (5)
☐ Controls in Balance	☐ All Equipment in Order
☐ Problems:	☐ Problems:

OTHER: *(Attendance, Supplies, New Production Jobs Accepted, Future Concerns, etc.)*

(6) ______________________________

(7) DATA PROCESSING MANAGER (8) DATE

INSTRUCTIONS FOR FORM:

OPERATIONS DAILY REPORT

DEFINITION OF EACH ELEMENT:

KEY	ELEMENT/CONTENT
1.	Recipient and Time Period This section identifies the recipient, the time period, and date that the report addresses.
2.	Communications Any comments about on-line or communications processes.
3.	Processing Comments on scheduled batch jobs.
4.	Input/Output/Tape Controls Comments about clerical control and tape-handling results.
5.	Equipment Performance Any comments about the adequacy of equipment performance and availability.
6.	Other Any additional remarks that may be appropriate to the processing period being reported upon, or matters of concern or interest to senior data processing management.
7.	Signature Signature of preparer.
8.	Date Date of preparation.

EXAMPLE

OPERATIONS DAILY REPORT

To: R. Yana

From: Data Processing Operations

PERFORMANCE FOR 8:00 PRIOR DAY TO 8:00 AM TODAY (Date) 3/14/XX

COMMUNICATIONS	PROCESSING
☐ Systems OK	☐ All Scheduled Jobs Run
☒ Problems:	☒ Incomplete Processing:
On-line late going up due to extended batch processing during 2nd & 3rd shift. Up at 8:00 a.m. instead of 6:00 a.m.	Job XBM003, Account Updates in loop due to missing term code. Will notify branch today to complete data. (See below)

INPUT/OUTPUT/TAPE CONTROLS	EQUIPMENT PERFORMANCE
☐ Controls in Balance	☒ All Equipment in Order
☒ Problems: G/L Balance off due to missing A/P data. Corrected and job rerun.	☐ Problems:

OTHER: *(Attendance, Supplies, New Production Jobs Accepted, Future Concerns, etc.)*

Re Processing - missing term data probably occurred during conversion where old files were not completely edited when created.

Running low on Statement forms - contacted forms supplier to rush.

Richard White
DATA PROCESSING MANAGER

3/14/XX
DATE

V

PROCEDURAL DOCUMENTATION

Procedural documentation provides management and clerical personnel with detailed instructions for operating and controlling a system. The specific objectives of this type of documentation are to:

- Provide a uniform source of reference on company policy and practices.
- Standardize clerical and operating routines in areas where standardization promotes efficiency.
- Aid in coordination of the operations and paperwork of two or more activities.
- Promote the input of complete and accurate data to the company's information systems.
- Provide a tool for training and supervision.
- Document methods for controlling company funds, property, and transactions in order to support the internal audit program.
- Assure systematic filing and retention of those company forms and records essential to sound business operations.

To remain useful and accurate, it is imperative that procedural documentation be maintained in concert with system modifications and enhancements. Procedural documentation updates are an integral part of systems maintenance activities. Procedural documentation consists of a separate procedures manual for each system. Each manual is typically composed of four major sections: table of contents, subject index, procedures, and exhibits. Each of these sections is briefly described below. A standard procedure format is recommended and is illustrated and described in the forms section. The forms section includes a sample of the standard procedure format, detailed instructions for its preparation, and examples of completed forms for table of contents, subject index, procedures, and exhibits.

Standard Procedures Manual

The purpose of a standard procedure format is to readily identify the subject, organizational areas involved, and specific functions covered, and to provide a climate of structure and organized approach for the work performed. The format accommodates the table of contents, subject index, procedures, and exhibits. (Figure 67)

Table of contents. The table of contents is a listing of all issued policies and procedures included in a system's procedures manual, showing procedure numbers and titles. (Figure 68)

Subject index. The subject index is an alphabetical procedures list. It contains procedure subsection headings and procedure and subsection numbers. (Figure 69)

Procedure. Procedures are written in modified playscript format. They describe the steps required for performing a single task or series of closely related tasks. (Figure 70)

Exhibits. Exhibits are copies of documents, reports, or CRT screen formats that are referenced in the procedures. These formats are included for clarification and information purposes. (Figure 71)

Figure 67
(Page 1 of 3)

STANDARD PROCEDURES MANUAL	DIVISION:
	DEPARTMENT:
	SECTION:
PROCEDURE NUMBER	PAGE:

ORIGINAL ISSUE DATE:	REVISIONS: / / /
APPROVAL SIGNATURE (S):	

Figure 67
(Page 2 of 3)

STANDARD PROCEDURES MANUAL (1)	DIVISION: (3)
	DEPARTMENT: (4)
	SECTION: (5)
PROCEDURE NUMBER (2)	PAGE: (6)

(7)

ORIGINAL ISSUE DATE: (8)	REVISIONS: (9) / / /
APPROVAL SIGNATURE (S): (10)	

INSTRUCTIONS FOR FORM: STANDARD PROCEDURES MANUAL

DEFINITION OF EACH ELEMENT:

KEY	ELEMENT/CONTENT
1.	Title Area Subject of this procedure.
2.	Procedure Number Indicates the number associated with the procedure title.
3.	Division Indicates the organizational entity or subsidiary to which the procedure applies.
4.	Department Specific department to which the procedure applies.
5.	Section Specific section or function within the department to which the procedure applies.
6.	Page Indicates the page sequence and total number.
7.	Text Area Identifies the tasks to be performed and who has authority for execution of the task. Also used for table of contents, subject index, and exhibits.
8.	Original Issue Date Date the procedure was issued.
9.	Revisions Dates of subsequent revisions.
10.	Approval Signature(s) Identifies approving authority. Includes subsequent signatures for revisions.

Figure 68

EXAMPLE

STANDARD PROCEDURES MANUAL	
ACCOUNTS PAYABLE CONTENTS	DIVISION: OPERATIONS
	DEPARTMENT: FINANCE
	SECTION: ACCOUNTS PAYABLE
PROCEDURE NUMBER TABLE OF CONTENTS	PAGE: 1 of 21

ORIGINAL ISSUE DATE: 8/3/XX	REVISIONS: / / /
APPROVAL SIGNATURE(S):	

EXAMPLE

Figure 69

STANDARD PROCEDURES MANUAL	DIVISION: OPERATIONS
ACCOUNTS PAYABLE SUBJECT INDEX	DEPARTMENT: FINANCE
	SECTION: ACCOUNTS PAYABLE
PROCEDURE NUMBER SUBJECT INDEX	PAGE: 2 of 21

ORIGINAL ISSUE DATE: 8/3/XX	REVISIONS: / / /
APPROVAL SIGNATURE (S):	

EXAMPLE

STANDARD PROCEDURES MANUAL	
ACCOUNTS PAYABLE PUBLICATION BILL PROCESSING	DIVISION: OPERATIONS DEPARTMENT: FINANCE SECTION: ACCOUNTS PAYABLE
PROCEDURE NUMBER AP-20	PAGE: 6 of 21

A. Processing Publication Invoices for Payment

Auditor

1. Receive publication invoices and supporting tear sheets from the mail room.
2. Prepare an Invoice/Tear Sheet Request (Exhibit P-10) for any missing tear sheets or invoices. Forward original to publication with copy of invoice or tear sheet received. Copy of Request is maintained in a Request Tickler File.
3. Sort invoices into the following sequence:
   - o Client
   - o Media
4. Compare each invoice to its respective Payer's List. The Payer's List shows the publications and insertions that are stored in the file, the space units, insertion dates and payable date. This is used to determine what publications need to be paid that month and the date they need to be paid to earn any cash discount that might be involved.
5. Verify the following data on the invoice to the Payer's List as follows:
   - o Media
   - o Client
   - o Product

ORIGINAL ISSUE DATE: 8/3/XX	REVISIONS: / / /
APPROVAL SIGNATURE (S):	

EXAMPLE

Figure 71

STANDARD PROCEDURES MANUAL	DIVISION: OPERATIONS
ACCOUNTS PAYABLE EXHIBITS	DEPARTMENT: FINANCE
	SECTION: ACCOUNTS PAYABLE
PROCEDURE NUMBER AP-50	PAGE: 19 of 21

EXHIBIT 10

New York, New York ..

212

INVOICE/TEARSHEET REQUEST

Client: ____________________

Issue Date: ____________________

Space Unit: ____________________

Gentlemen:

We have not as yet received your invoice for the above insertion and would like to pay you so we can balance out our records.

If the insertion did not run, please note this on the bottom of this letter and return to me so that we can delete it from our records.

If it did run, please send me an invoice and tearsheet for the ad, addressed to my personal attention, so that we can process it for payment.

It is understood that we will be granted the normal terms of payment and all deductions/cash discounts allowed since any default in payment is not ours, but due to non-receipt of your invoice.

Thanks for your cooperation and quick attention to this matter.

Sincerely,

____

Telephone (212, ______

Date ____________________

Comments:

ORIGINAL ISSUE DATE: 8/3/XX	REVISIONS: / / /
APPROVAL SIGNATURE (S):	

NOTES

NOTES

NOTES

NOTES

NOTES